ANOTHER 100 GREATEST CYCLING CLIMBS

A ROAD CYCLIST'S GUIDE TO BRITAIN'S HILLS

D1426802

F

FRANCES LINCOLN LIMITED
PUBLISHERS

Frances Lincoln Limited
4 Torriano Mews
Torriano Avenue
London NW5 2RZ
www.franceslincoln.com

Another 100 Greatest Cycling Climbs:
A Road Cyclist's Guide to Britain's Hills
Copyright © Frances Lincoln Limited 2012
Text, photographs, design and illustrations copyright © Simon Warren 2012

First Frances Lincoln edition 2012

A catalogue record for this book is available from the British Library.

978-0-7112-3265-5

Printed and bound in China

1 2 3 4 5 6 7 8 9

FOR MUM AND DAD

20%

Hill steepens
lowest gear
now

Cyclists
advised
to walk

CONTENTS

WELCOME BACK

First of all, I have to apologize to all those people who've only just started to tick off the climbs in the first book, I've gone and doubled your work load. For those of you who've already bagged the first 100 then I'm just in time, but if you think you're in for an easier ride this time round then think again. Just because these climbs are listed 101 to 200, every one of them would, or could have made volume one. They are all rated to the same standard, a 10 out of 10 is still a 10 out of 10, and wow, have I found some awesome roads.

I say found, because, unlike the more familiar climbs in volume one, the majority in this book I was riding for the first time and it's been a fantastic 18 months of adventure and discovery. From dark and twisting lanes in the tip of Cornwall to mountainesque passes in the Highlands of Scotland. From being roughed up by the weather in the Pennines, to being relentlessly worn down by the slopes of the North York Moors. I've travelled the length and breadth of the nation in search of gradient and for a number of entries I've gone a little further off the beaten track. I've thrown in a few curve balls, not roads you'd normally fit into a weekend ride but killer climbs you just have to see to believe. I ventured offshore for the first time too, to the Isle of Man and had the best day on a bike I can

remember, it's great riding country.

I've just about squeezed in all the roads it pained me to leave out of volume one and I hope I've included all the climbs you were disappointed not to have seen first time round. The roads whose exclusion left you outraged and dismayed, well, fingers crossed they are all here. But if not, then I need to know what's missing, a real monster I've overlooked then tweet me (@100Climbs) and I'll check it out as soon as I can.

Back to this book. You may be wondering how I can claim volume two to be Longer! Higher! and Steeper! than volume one. Well, 'Longer' belongs to Cragg Vale, the longest continuous uphill gradient in the whole of England. Higher, 'Higher' belongs to what has become my new favourite climb, the road up to the radar station on top of Great Dun Fell. In my opinion this is the single greatest ascent in the whole of Britain, greater even than Bealach-na-Ba. Of all the climbs, from 1 to 200 I urge you, if you love a challenge, to go give it a try. Finally, 'Steeper', Steeper belongs to Vale Street in Bristol, the steepest and craziest residential road in Europe, a bit of a novelty yes, but who am I to argue with the facts.

So here it is then, more 30% hairpin corners, more jagged cobbles, more barren moors and another 100 reasons to just get out and ride. Have fun.

LEAN, CLEAN AND MEAN

My obsession with lightweight bikes began in May 1990 with the purchase of one of my most treasured possessions. Whilst on a family holiday in the USA, I picked up a copy of a magazine called *Bicycle Guide* and that month it just happened to be 'The light weight issue'.

The whole magazine was devoted to the lightest new bikes, saving weight, and best of all, lightweight exotica. Compared to today's world of carbon fibre, the lightweight market in the early 1990s was in its infancy, and the major manufacturers were just starting to experiment with new technologies and materials. There were a few innovative companies, however, who had been pushing the envelope for a number of years and they had created products that I'd heard rumour about but never seen in the flesh. That was until, on a spread of the magazine, they were all laid out in front of me. I drooled over the beautiful components, the 16 mm Assos rims, the Campagnolo alloy freewheel, and

there, amongst the unaffordable and unobtainable were a pair of Mavic alloy skewers. I did a double take, I already owned a pair of these, suddenly this lightweight dream was accessible, suddenly I was in the game.

Another item on the page was a pair of Vitus Duralinox forks, at the time the 'lightest production bonded aluminum fork available'. When I returned home it was 'conveniently' time to upgrade my race bike, I checked out the Vitus frames and amazingly they were very reasonably priced, pound for gram they were the best deal out there. Detractors said they flexed too much, and if you crashed they would crumple like a tin can, but I was sold. I was only interested in weight and anyhow I was too light to flex anything and didn't have any plans to crash.

Then as with now, the greatest barrier preventing a rider having the lightest possible bike is cash. I'd blown all I had on the new frame. Thankfully I already had a very nice set of wheels so what else could I do now the bank account was empty. As I started racing hill climbs I'd look closely at the other riders' bikes, especially Chris Boardman's. His attention to detail was famous and his machines would

May 1990 *Bicycle Guide*.

Chris Boardman's 1992 bike (left) and my early 1990s attempt to save as much weight as possible.

always be immaculate, nothing was overlooked. The one that really sticks in my mind is the one he used during his 1992 campaign (above). It was so neat, from the sloping top tube to the state of the art lightweight Zipp disc. He'd even cut the drops off his bars as they were surplus to requirements, and this got me thinking. What could I take off my bike that I didn't need, how could I shave a precious few grams off for free?

And so started a ritual that I continue to this day. At the end of the road season, as the leaves begin to fall I take everything off the bike that I don't need for climbing yet still stay within the rules. First I take

off the big ring and the front changer, then I remove a few links from the chain because it doesn't need to stretch as far. I remove the bottle cages, the bolts and the computer, but unlike Boardman I can't chop my bars off each year, that just isn't financially viable. Instead I take half the bar tape off, this saves at best 10 grams, but gives the impression that the bars have been cropped. Does all this tinkering really make a difference? Every single gram you remove should tip the equation in your favour, so hopefully it does.

But it's more than just the weight saving, it's the preparation, it's being ready, doing all you can with what you

A lightweight masterpiece

have. Take for example the bike to the left. Belonging to the prolific hill climber Rob English, every component has been hand-picked, modified or personalized. From the tiny carbon frame, the single chain ring, and the paper thin tyres, to the lack of bar tape, bespoke wheels and the carbon saddle. It's a work of art, built for one purpose, to race up hills. ▶▶

So what can you do to your machine? How can you save some weight to help you in the fight against the evils of gravity? I mentioned before that I already had a pair of very nice wheels. If you are ever looking to improve your ride the wheels are the first and singularly most important component you should seek to improve. If the frame is the heart of the bike then the wheels are its lungs. A good light set of wheels will quite literally transform any bike and there's even some real science to back it up.

Rotational weight, to be found concentrated in the rims, is worth, according to physics, twice that of static weight such as the weight of the frame. This phenomenon is especially evident during acceleration, so this is where you must focus your attention, and more than likely, your bank balance. The overwhelming majority of today's wheels come factory built as an integral unit so it isn't as easy to upgrade just the rims. You will be forced to replace the wheels and you are spoilt for choice. There's a set available at every price point between £100 and £5,000, with the pound per gram saved increasing exponentially.

Back in 1990, however, building a lightweight set of wheels was a whole different ball game. It started with trawling studiously through the classifieds for the constituent parts. I set my heart on a pair of 28-hole Wolber Profile 18 mm V section rims, not only were they 'aero' but they tipped the scales at a fraction over 300 grams each and this was exceptional

1970s drilling beauty

for the day. Once found, I matched them with a pair of the smoothest hubs available, some Mavic 501s and sent them off to my trusted wheel builder for construction. Lightweight wheel building was a journey then, it needed knowledge, involved a search, and was finished off with craftsmanship. This approach is still available for those with very deep pockets, but simply not necessary as the ready-built products are so good. It's a shame in a way that the heart and soul have been removed somewhat from the lightweight battle. Gone are the days when, in order to make your bike lighter than your neighbour's you took to the shed with the drill. Also covered in the same issue of *Bicycle Guide* (above) the practice of drilling involved removing every last bit of metal that wasn't structurally essential for the component to work. The aim being to strike the exact balance between weight and a catastrophic mid-ride accident.

So go to the garage, study your bike, remove any and all excess clutter, upgrade what you can afford, and always keep it clean! lean! and mean!

LEGEND

UNDERSTANDING THE FACTFILES AND RATINGS

LOCATIONS

You will be able to locate each hill from the small maps, simply, **S** marks the start and **F** marks the finish. I would suggest you invest in either Ordnance Survey maps or a GPS system to help plan your routes in more detail. The grid reference in the factfile locates the summit of each climb and in brackets is the relevant **OS Landranger** map. The graphic at the start of each chapter will show you where the hills lie in the context of each region.

TIMINGS

Each factfile includes the approximate time needed to ride each hill. Timed over the distance marked, this is how long it took me to complete each climb at a reasonable, but comfortable pace. Since I rode in all weathers from blizzards to baking heat, I have adjusted the times slightly to accommodate for the adverse conditions I faced on the day. The times could be used as a target but are really just intended as a rough guide.

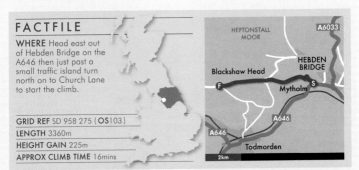

FACTFILE

WHERE Head east out of Hebden Bridge on the A646 then just past a small traffic island turn north on to Church Lane to start the climb.

GRID REF SD 958 275 (**OS**103)

LENGTH 3360m

HEIGHT GAIN 225m

APPROX CLIMB TIME 16mins

RATINGS

The climbs are rated from **1/10** to **10/10** within the context of the book. The rating is an amalgamation of gradient, length, the likely hostility of the riding conditions and the condition of the surface. All the climbs are tough, therefore **1/10** equals 'hard', and **10/10** equals 'it's all you can do to keep your bike moving'. Some will suit you more than others, the saying 'horses for courses' applies, but all the **10/10** climbs will test any rider.

MAP KEY

Motorway	M1
A Road	A123
B Road	B1234
Minor Road	
Rail line	STATION
Hill route	S START ——— F FINISH
Town	TOWN
Scale	2km

ORIGIN OF THE TTs

Mention the V718 or the L812 to any time trialist and they will instantly understand what you're talking about. Why? Because they are course codes, an essential part of the tradition and quirkiness of the sport. They may seem to the outsider an archaic way of describing a certain stretch of tarmac, and they appear to defy all logic, but without them the sport of time trialling would not exist today. Turn the clock back to the late 1890s and British cycling was in turmoil, the National Cyclists' Union had been forced to take the bold step to ban all racing on public roads. This was to pre-empt the enforcement of a ban by motorists' groups, on all cycling full stop. Cyclists were a menace, said to terrorise motorists, bunch races were sabotaged and on occasion halted by police on horse back charging at the peloton, thrusting sticks into riders' wheels. Not to be undone though, and led by men such as Frederick Thomas Bidlake, an ingenious system was devised to allow racing without attracting the attention of either motorists or the law. The time trial was born. Riders would start at minute intervals, at the crack of dawn, dressed head to toe in black, leaving from a pre-arranged, but most importantly, unpublished location. It was this need to keep the locations secret that created the most unusual of all the time trial peculiarities, the course codes.

They appear utterly random if you scan through the back of the CTT handbook, and for the most part they are. The nation was split up into divisions, and each division developed it's own system, and conveniently no two are the same. This helps to keep them hidden allright, but makes them all but impossible to decipher. In the case of hill climbs, the majority of courses are named after the roads they run up so the need for a code was even more relevant. In some regions you will often find an H in the moniker, and in a couple even an HC! In Yorkshire, however, where all courses begin with a V, the denotation of a hill climb comes in the next two numbers, which are either 89 or 99. Complicated? Yes. 100% British idiosyncrasy? Yes. And may they forever be a part of the fabric of our sport.

HILL CLIMB CODES

KH27	Dovers Hill
S49/HC	Peak Hill
GH/31	White Lane
GH/32	Yorks Hill
BHC/1	Semer Hill
AHC/1	Riber Bank
OHC3	Monsal Head
OHC6	Rowsley Bank
V9920	Halifax Lane
V9916	Cragg Vale
OHC9	Pea Royd Lane
V9912	Jackson Bridge
V897	Norwood Edge
THC4	Carlton Bank
L806	Nick O'Pendle
L812	The Rake
L820	Jubilee Tower
J9/14	Mow Cop
J9/7	Cat & Fiddle
DO/1	Horseshoe Pass

CHECK YOUR **BIKE**, CHECK YOUR **BODY**, AND ALWAYS WEAR A **HELMET**.

Many of the roads in this book cross the wildest and most inhospitable parts of the nation. You'll often find yourself in open and exposed country so have a good look at the weather forecast before you head out. Although far from impossible most of the climbs require a good level of fitness so only attempt the really tough ones if you are confident of your ability. Remember that what goes up at 1-in-4 is also likely to come down at 1-in-4 so check your brakes and most of all have fun.

SOUTH-WEST

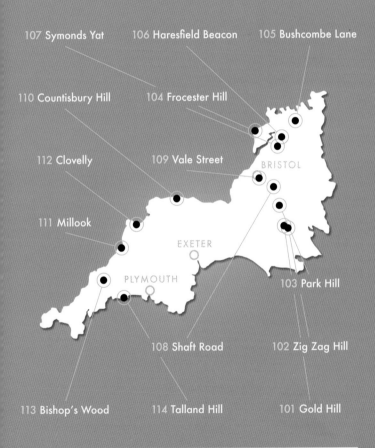

107 Symonds Yat
106 Haresfield Beacon
105 Bushcombe Lane
110 Countisbury Hill
104 Frocester Hill
112 Clovelly
109 Vale Street
BRISTOL
111 Millook
EXETER
PLYMOUTH
103 Park Hill
108 Shaft Road
102 Zig Zag Hill
113 Bishop's Wood
114 Talland Hill
101 Gold Hill

RATING 7/10

101 GOLD HILL

Gold Hill is the centrepiece of the most picture-perfect chocolate box scene in the whole of Britain. Immortalized by the famous Hovis Bread TV ad, the view from the top attracts visitors from every corner of the globe. So if you're going to attempt this climb then beware, as soon as you begin your ascent you too will become part of the attraction. Your every strained revolution will be scrutinized as your effort becomes entertainment – you dare not fail to reach the top now. Starting at the junction with Layton Lane, following a brief stretch of tarmac the cobbles begin; it is extremely steep and the stones are also greasy and uneven so to aid traction try to stay seated. To make matters worse, every 10 metres or so you cross a ridge of larger stones that hit you like waves. You will be constantly forced to find the better line, as if navigating an uphill maze, to finish in the small sloping plaza in front of the café.

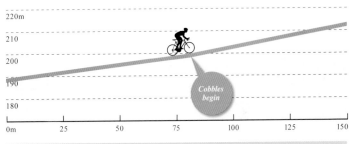

Cobbles begin

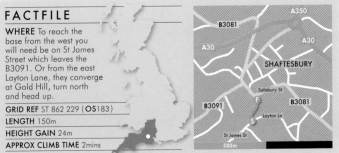

FACTFILE

WHERE To reach the base from the west you will need be on St James Street which leaves the B3091. Or from the east Layton Lane, they converge at Gold Hill, turn north and head up.

GRID REF ST 862 229 (OS183)

LENGTH 150m

HEIGHT GAIN 24m

APPROX CLIMB TIME 2mins

102 ZIG ZAG HILL

Just south of Shaftesbury sit the sweeping tangled bends of Zig Zag Hill. This mini-mountainesque ascent is perfect for riders wanting to hone their uphill cornering technique before heading off to the Alps or the Pyrenees. Beginning where the tarmac changes colour, the surface is really rugged and there are also deep-set iron grilles to avoid. The first of the three hairpins is a tight right-hander, the next a left – through this the road bends right, tight left, right and into the third hairpin. Ride smoothly into the bends, as the road levels slightly don't change up, spin the small gear, offer the legs a short rest then build a fraction more momentum before you exit and begin to push again. The slopes are steepest at the bottom, but not outrageous at 10%. Round a final sweeping left-hand bend and you exit the trees to ride the smooth upper slopes into Wiltshire to summit at the brow, just past a large car park on your right.

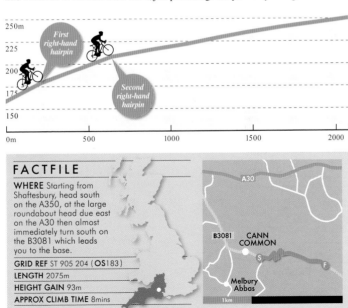

FACTFILE

WHERE Starting from Shaftesbury, head south on the A350, at the large roundabout head due east on the A30 then almost immediately turn south on the B3081 which leads you to the base.

GRID REF ST 905 204 (OS183)

LENGTH 2075m

HEIGHT GAIN 93m

APPROX CLIMB TIME 8mins

103 PARK HILL

Park Hill is set in the grounds of Longleat Park, the base sitting adjacent to the magnificent stately home. It feels slightly unnatural to be riding your bike in such a pristine setting but it is a public right of way, the road goes up and the tarmac is all but perfect. Begin across a cattle grid, looking up ahead the road appears to have been gently draped over the manicured grassy banks. There's no hedge or wall, no boundary between you and the well-kept grass dotted with neatly placed groups of trees. Levelling past the second cattle grid as you approach a 90-degree left-hand bend and the road climbs, steeply. The hardest climbing is at the end, burning legs are burning legs whether they are on a windswept Welsh mountain or within the confines of a giant landscaped garden. There's no escaping the effort involved in reaching the top as this is a serious climb in a somewhat bizarre but almost traffic-free environment.

FACTFILE

WHERE Enter Longleat Park and make your way to Longleat House. Start the ascent heading east from the bridge between Half Mile Pond and Ford Pond.

GRID REF ST 825 433 (OS183)

LENGTH 1740m

HEIGHT GAIN 127m

APPROX CLIMB TIME 8mins

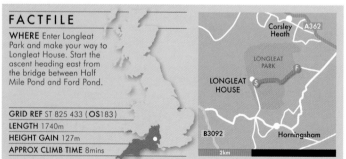

FROCESTER, GLOUCESTERSHIRE

A beautiful sweeping ascent with stunning views all the way up, never too steep but always a test – a perfect climb. Start the ascent from the crossroads at the centre of Frocester and roll out on the gentle well-surfaced road. Past the village sign, although not steep yet, you're now on the hill; up above, the perfect grassy banks appear shaven, topped with a head of woodland hair. Passing a 10% sign the road kinks right, the surface now rougher eases a bit then rises again taking you through a well-marked left-hander into a long straight. The gradient is all but uniform, steep, but it's never a grind, you pass through a large S-bend, kinking first right then left, that takes the road via a giant arc into the shelter of the trees at the top. The surface a bit rougher now, the road eventually deviates from its constant gradient then eases before finishing abruptly at the junction with the B4066.

FACTFILE

WHERE Find your way to Frocester, from the crossroads in the centre of the village, ride south up the ridge to the B4066.

GRID REF SO 794 004 (OS162)

LENGTH 3100m

HEIGHT GAIN 203m

APPROX CLIMB TIME 14mins

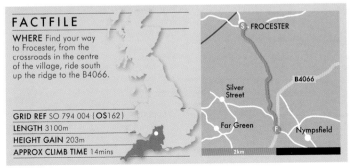

105 BUSHCOMBE LANE

WOODMANCOTE, GLOUCESTERSHIRE

You're spoilt for choice when it comes to climbing Cleeve Hill. The three vicious ascents leaving Woodmancote all offer a fantastic challenge, and of the three it's Bushcombe Lane that stands apart. From the junction with Station Road, exit the village past the first 25% sign then the road bends left at a second 25% warning – as if you need reminding, it's going to be hard. Once the gradient kicks in it just gets steeper and steeper, 20% past the last of the houses, then the fun really starts. Banking right, the surface breaks up and 20% soon turns into 25%. This is one of the toughest bits of road anywhere in the UK and, through the next left-hand bend, it touches 30% at the apex. Heave yourself round this evil corner and you're through the worst of it. There is still some way to go but you can click through the gears before finishing just after a gaping cattle grid adjacent to a small car park.

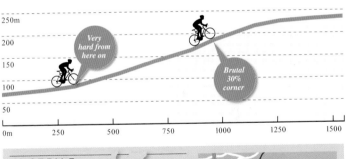

Very hard from here on

Brutal 30% corner

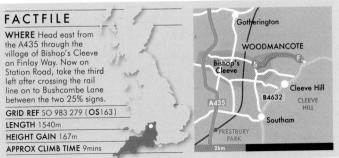

FACTFILE

WHERE Head east from the A435 through the village of Bishop's Cleeve on Finlay Way. Now on Station Road, take the third left after crossing the rail line on to Bushcombe Lane between the two 25% signs.

GRID REF SO 983 279 (OS163)

LENGTH 1540m

HEIGHT GAIN 167m

APPROX CLIMB TIME 9mins

HARESFIELD, GLOUCESTERSHIRE

A climb that starts in the pleasant surroundings of Haresfield village but soon turns nasty on a wicked stretch of 20% gradient. Ease your way out of the village up Beacon Road to the first test, a collection of smooth, winding bends framed by high hedgerows. These early twists and turns aren't particularly fierce, but will more than likely have you leaving your saddle. Exiting the final bend you ride up to a group of farmhouses where you're allowed to catch your breath slightly. Make the most of this because here comes the steep bit, an unforgiving ramp up a rough surface under the cover of trees. This 20% torment ends at a pronounced lump in the tarmac and, as the trees retreat, you can now sit back down to ride the gentle slope up to the next brow. This, alas, isn't the summit but what follows is even gentler and you finally peak adjacent to two large concrete bails in a field entrance on your left.

FACTFILE

WHERE Leave the B4008 travelling south out of Gloucester, then head south-east on the minor road from Hardwicke. Cross the M5, then the railway bridge, then turn right in front of the school to reach the base.

GRID REF SO 830 086 (OS162)

LENGTH 2350m

HEIGHT GAIN 200m

APPROX CLIMB TIME 12mins

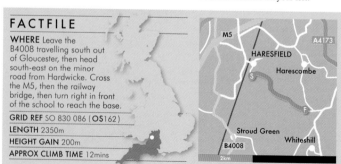

SYMONDS YAT, HEREFORDSHIRE

Just inside the English border on the edge of the Forest of Dean lies Symonds Yat Rock sitting on a thumb-shaped island surrounded by the River Wye. The wonderful climb to the top of this mound starts on the flat plain at the gates to Huntsman Court, underneath an artistic metal stag's head sitting on a gatepost. It's gentle to begin with up to the 'Welcome to Symonds Yat East' sign, then as you climb up through the trees it soon gets hard, approaching 17% in places. You break out of the trees into a brief clearing where the slope eases slightly before sending you back under more trees and more of the same tough gradient. Just past the small village with its beautiful stone houses you hit the hardest slopes. It's a proper, tough 20% slog up to the finish. Keep focused on the wooden footbridge that crosses high above the road just shy of the brow, head under it and it's over.

FACTFILE

WHERE Leave the B4229 south of Goodrich and head south on the minor road across the River Wye. Ride along the flat, pass a few houses and start at the elaborate stag on the gatepost on your left.

GRID REF SO 563 159 (**OS**162)

LENGTH 1800m

HEIGHT GAIN 116m

APPROX CLIMB TIME 8mins

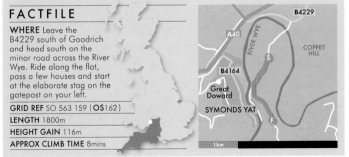

108 SHAFT ROAD

COMBE DOWN, BATH

Originally I'd intended to include Brassknocker Hill to the east, but after riding it I was put off by the amount of traffic I encountered. Disappointed, I decided to take a look at Shaft Road on the same ridge – would this be a brilliant climb? What a discovery – it was quiet, filled with twists, flanked by beautiful stone walls and best of all, tougher than Brassknocker. Start the climb at the T-junction in the village of Monkton Combe, 20 metres in, and keep right as the road forks. The climbing is steady as you leave the village behind then rears up after a sharp left-hand bend and into a cover of trees. Once through this stretch you approach some houses, levelling as you do, then kicking up afterwards, not lethal, but about 17%. It continues tough for some distance, snaking between the neat stone walls up to a 90-degree right-hander, still tough through the bend then gently regressing to finish outside Bay Tree House on the right.

FACTFILE

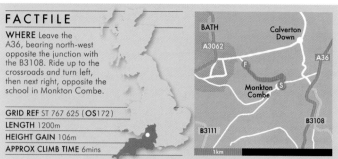

WHERE Leave the A36, bearing north-west opposite the junction with the B3108. Ride up to the crossroads and turn left, then next right, opposite the school in Monkton Combe.

GRID REF ST 767 625 (**OS**172)

LENGTH 1200m

HEIGHT GAIN 106m

APPROX CLIMB TIME 6mins

TOTTERDOWN, BRISTOL

OK, it's no stunning mountain pass, and little more than a novelty, but Vale Street is the steepest residential road in Europe. This corner of Bristol may not be top of your list of cycling destinations but it is a playground of ultra steep roads. From afar the houses look as if they are stacked on top of each other, and hidden among them is Vale Street. At first glance it looks impossible, and I'd say on the left-hand side of the road it is – instead of a pavement on that side there's a flight of stairs as it rears abruptly from Park Street. You're going to need a serious run up. The thing is, Park Street is all but 20%, so just try to gather what speed you can, turn left and commit. Your nerves will be racing and you will have to give it 100%. Head for the right-hand side of the road and hit it hard. It will take you a matter of seconds to conquer and once through the first 10 metres you're safe – bag it, and then spend a few hours on the surrounding streets.

FACTFILE

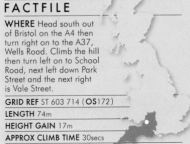

WHERE Head south out of Bristol on the A4 then turn right on to the A37, Wells Road. Climb the hill then turn left on to School Road, next left down Park Street and the next right is Vale Street.

GRID REF ST 603 714 (**OS**172)

LENGTH 74m

HEIGHT GAIN 17m

APPROX CLIMB TIME 30secs

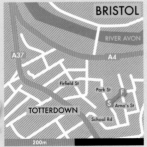

LYNMOUTH, DEVON

One of three great climbs that leave Lynmouth, Countisbury Hill takes you east offering fantastic views out over the Bristol Channel. Begin the climb immediately as you leave town and it's straight up. The sign says 25% as you head into darkness under the trees, but this seems a bit of an exaggeration, it feels more like 20%. As you exit the trees into daylight overlooking Lynmouth Bay, you're through the toughest stretch and, legs burning, you see your next task ahead of you. The long, steady climb, coarsely surfaced, makes it heavy going, but once your legs have recovered from the abrupt start the even gradient will allow you to find a good rhythm. The route snakes left and right as it follows the coastline, climbing all the time as you approach Countisbury, then levels, dips, then rears once more. This time up to 16% delivering you into the final long push to the top at the apex of a sweeping left-hand bend.

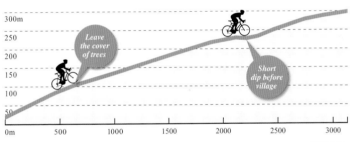

Leave the cover of trees

Short dip before village

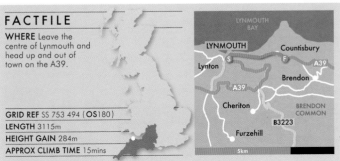

FACTFILE

WHERE Leave the centre of Lynmouth and head up and out of town on the A39.

GRID REF SS 753 494 (OS180)
LENGTH 3115m
HEIGHT GAIN 284m
APPROX CLIMB TIME 15mins

111 MILLOOK

MILLOOK, CORNWALL

I couldn't wait to ride this climb. Any road rated 30% gets my pulse racing and I felt like a kid on my way to Disneyland as I rode south from Bude. Upon arrival I discovered not one, but two 30% ascents. Which would I choose for the book? I could pick just one, so I chose the route south. Although it lacks the dramatic final corner of the route north it is, all things considered, the tougher challenge. Bending left away from the bridge at the base you're almost instantly faced with a 30% corner – but what follows is worse. You are delivered into a remorseless stretch of 20% climbing, you'll be at your maximum and need to recover but it's just not possible. On and on, steeper still in the corners. It is now just about survival. Although easing slightly in places, the final rise will take everything you've got. Keep your focus on the brow, reach this and although it's not quite the top, you're safe and can relax.

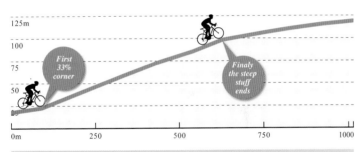

First 33% corner

Finaly the steep stuff ends

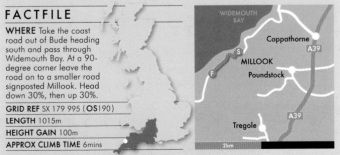

FACTFILE

WHERE Take the coast road out of Bude heading south and pass through Widemouth Bay. At a 90-degree corner leave the road on to a smaller road signposted Millook. Head down 30%, then up 30%.

GRID REF SX 179 995 (OS190)

LENGTH 1015m

HEIGHT GAIN 100m

APPROX CLIMB TIME 6mins

WIDEMOUTH BAY

Coppathorne

A39

S

MILLOOK

Poundstock

F

A39

Tregole

2km

112 CLOVELLY

CLOVELLY, DEVON

It's not possible to ride the cobbled streets of the proudly traffic free Clovelly, but there is a road you can ride – the incredibly steep, private access route that's used by 4x4s to ferry the many visitors to and from the shore. You'll be going out of your way to find this hill but it's more than worth the detour if you're a fan of the steep stuff. Confronted by numerous 'traffic free' signs I asked the car park attendant if I was allowed to ride down, 'Of course,' he said, 'but you'll not be able to ride back up no matter how fit you are.' My eyes narrowed, and I raced down to the bottom. Once at the base, engage your largest sprocket and hit the slope that starts immediately at 20%. It's a dark, rough single carriageway road that offers little if no respite. Where you can have a breather take it, as the higher it gets the harder it gets. The upper slopes with daylight breaking through the canopy might even touch 30% on the bends. What a road.

FACTFILE

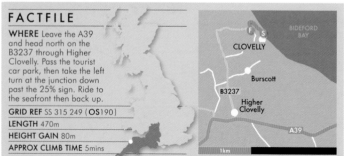

WHERE Leave the A39 and head north on the B3237 through Higher Clovelly. Pass the tourist car park, then take the left turn at the junction down past the 25% sign. Ride to the seafront then back up.

GRID REF SS 315 249 (OS190)

LENGTH 470m

HEIGHT GAIN 80m

APPROX CLIMB TIME 5mins

BURLAWN, CORNWALL

Hidden in a dark labyrinth of narrow twisting lanes south of Wadebridge lies the climb of Bishop's Wood. It's remarkably easy to get lost around here; the lack of landmarks in the shadowy lanes can easily disorientate you. When you do finally find the base in the thick woodland I'm betting by the time you reach the top you'll wish you hadn't. Start as you cross the stream, round the bend, pass the first 28% warning sign and then keep left at the fork. If you can climb this next stretch of road you'll pretty much be able to climb anything. Viciously steep, strewn with gravel and debris, punctuated by momentum-sapping ridges it's a perfect storm of obstacles. A large lump in the tarmac marks the end of the steepest stretch. It's still very hard after this, 20%, easing back, then 20% again. But it does eventually abate and after numerous kinks right and left, you'll eventually reach the summit of Cornwall's hidden beast.

FACTFILE

WHERE Head south of Wadebridge and find your way into Burlawn. Snake east out of the village, right at a phone box and continue down into the gully, cross a small bridge and you're at the base.

GRID REF SX 008 694 (OS200)

LENGTH 325m

HEIGHT GAIN 47m

APPROX CLIMB TIME 5mins

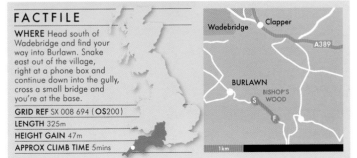

RATING 10/10

114 TALLAND HILL

POLPERRO, CORNWALL

Bold 'no entry' signs greet you at the base. Obviously these are intended to halt those with motor vehicles, no one would attempt to ride up Talland Hill on a bike would they? The perfection this road offers to those in search of the nation's toughest gradients is matched only by the beauty of the Cornish fishing village at its base. There's scant room for a run up amid the tourists, but get what you can, stick it in your biggest sprocket and attack. Not since I ascended Hardknott and Wrynose have I been forced to ride such a distance out of the saddle, but still, it's never a chore. Through the neatly painted houses on either side it's all but dead straight and doesn't back off an inch until you reach the wooded area halfway up. Pass the turn for the primary school and then you can relax for the final leg almost to the T-junction at the top, then turn left, head back down into town and ride it again, it's impossible not to – it's that good.

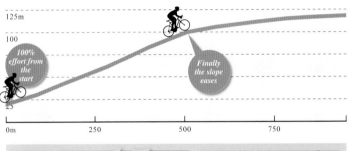

125m

100

100% effort from the start

Finally the slope eases

25

0m   250   500   750

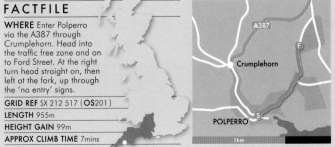

FACTFILE

WHERE Enter Polperro via the A387 through Crumplehorn. Head into the traffic free zone and on to Ford Street. At the right turn head straight on, then left at the fork, up through the 'no entry' signs.

GRID REF SX 212 517 (**OS**201)

LENGTH 955m

HEIGHT GAIN 99m

APPROX CLIMB TIME 7mins

A387

Crumplehorn

F

POLPERRO   S

1km

SOUTH-EAST

121 Dragon Hill Road

122 Kingston Hill

118 Coldharbour Lane

116 Combe Lane

117 Chalkpit Lane

OXFORD

LONDON

PORTSMOUTH

115 Ashdown Forest

123 Down Lane

119 Quell Lane

120 Barhatch Lane

GROOMBRIDGE, EAST SUSSEX

If you leave Groombridge in a large group of riders, heading to the top of Ashdown Forest, it fast becomes survival of the fittest as each ridge takes its toll. The climb's strength is the sum of its parts, it's a war of attrition that requires concentration and willpower to conquer. Exit Groombridge then turn south on to the B2188, dip down under a railway bridge and start the climb in the hollow. Your first rise is a stinging ramp before a short, fast descent to the base of the next ridge. Climb up to a junction on the left and continue on to pass through Friars Gate, on and on under the trees, getting steeper in places forcing you to grit your teeth a little. The first sign that you're getting close to the top is the large clearing where the sky opens up, cross this exposed stretch then plunge back under tree cover where the slope really kicks up. You then level for a brief rest before it kicks up into the last steep bit before you make your way to the top.

FACTFILE

WHERE Head south out of Groombridge on the B2110 then at the junction take the B2188 signposted Crowborough. Duck down under the railway bridge then head up from the hollow.

GRID REF TQ 477 310 (OS188)

LENGTH 7500m

HEIGHT GAIN 174m

APPROX CLIMB TIME 21mins

GROOMBRIDGE

Hartfield

Upper Hartfield

Withyham

B2110

B2026

Friar's Gate

A26

B2188

Crowborough

B2100

5km

116 COMBE LANE

A much kinder ride up the North Downs than the infamous White Downs, a couple of miles to the east, but nonetheless one with a real sting in its tail. Leave the village of Shere from its western exit, cross the A25 and the climb starts straight away from the main road. It doesn't hit you right away, you've plenty of time to get used to the incline, up to the first serious bends, first left then right, then you know you're climbing. You've now a long straight and up ahead you see the road bend right and climbing is noticeably tougher. You'll now need to click up a couple of sprockets to preserve a good cadence and continue to bend right pushing on up to the hairpin. This is where you'll need to get out of the saddle and give it everything round into the final short stretch. It's a super-tough left-hand bend into a super-tough ramp. Follow the road up to the sharp right-hand corner and then finish at the brow where the slope ebbs away.

FACTFILE

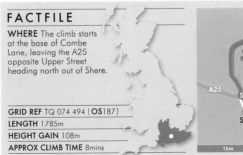

WHERE The climb starts at the base of Combe Lane, leaving the A25 opposite Upper Street heading north out of Shere.

GRID REF TQ 074 494 (**OS**187)	
LENGTH 1785m	
HEIGHT GAIN 108m	
APPROX CLIMB TIME 8mins	

117 CHALKPIT LANE

LIMPSFIELD, SURREY

My favourite climb in the south-east, it was a tough call to leave it out of volume one but here it is in all its glory. The climb is gentle at first as you leave Limpsfield but above you the vertical chalk face that dominates the skyline awaits. Make the most of the early slopes: they don't last. Passing beneath the monumental square bridge under the M25, the gradient starts to bite, still not terrible but enough to quicken the breathing and lower the gears. Bending left past the first entrance to the chalk pit you now know you're on a proper hill. Ahead, the wicked right-hand hairpin comes into view and from there begins the toughest stretch. Grind round the corner and begin an achingly uniform 20% slog on the perfectly surfaced road. Dead straight, you are offered no respite for over 200 metres before it gradually bends left and thankfully finishes at the T-junction.

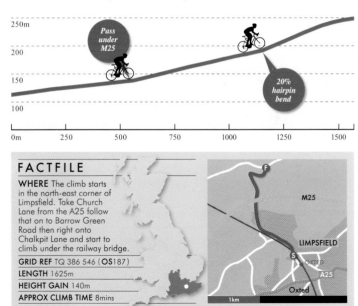

FACTFILE

WHERE The climb starts in the north-east corner of Limpsfield. Take Church Lane from the A25 follow that on to Barrow Green Road then right onto Chalkpit Lane and start to climb under the railway bridge.

GRID REF TQ 386 546 (OS187)

LENGTH 1625m

HEIGHT GAIN 140m

APPROX CLIMB TIME 8mins

Even on the brightest summer's day it's dark on Coldharbour Lane, lying at the bottom of a canyon-like trench lined with 5-metre-high dirt walls under a tall canopy of thick forest. From Dorking leave the A25 on to Falkland Road and then over a small bump before dropping to level past farm buildings, this is where the climb truly begins. Easing your way up the incline, it's hard, getting harder under the trees before easing off a little then hard again to the junction on the right. The claustrophobic banks are now growing around you and the road kinks slightly left to continue its gloomy journey along the debris-covered surface. The name of the road changes briefly past the junction, to Boar Hill, and this is the toughest stretch of climbing. As soon as the gradient recedes you return to Coldharbour Lane to continue the lumpy journey to the summit shortly before you roll down into Coldharbour itself.

FACTFILE

WHERE To reach the base follow the A25 'South Street' through Dorking. At the T-junction head left on to Falkland Road then immediately right on to Coldharbour Lane, ride up then down and start on the flat.

GRID REF TQ 156 449 (OS187)

LENGTH 3300m

HEIGHT GAIN 145m

APPROX CLIMB TIME 11mins

119 QUELL LANE

HASLEMERE, SURREY

RATING 4/10

I found myself in this corner of Surrey to ride up Fernden Lane south out of Haslemere but happened to approach it from the south and headed up Quell Lane. After weighing things up, and disregarding the superior length of Fernden Lane I decided Quell Lane was a more worthy inclusion. It's steeper, a purer climber's climb, and it's lined with some stunning properties, not that that should form part of the equation. Start steep, heading off at an angle from the main road then bend left before sweeping round to the right and backing off slightly. Next is the first real tough stretch, round to the left then into a sharp, straight ramp up to a left-hand bend and an easing. The surface is now rough, overspread with gravel, in fact there are enough stones in the centre to cover a modest driveway. Keep to the clean tarmac, up the second really tough grind, then follow the road round to the left and finish as Fernden Lane begins.

FACTFILE

WHERE Leave the A283 one junction south of the B2131 head east then turn left at Gospel Green onto Jobson's Lane. Take your third right on to Quell Lane and climb.

GRID REF SU 922 290 (**OS**186)	
LENGTH 1050m	
HEIGHT GAIN 88m	
APPROX CLIMB TIME 5mins	

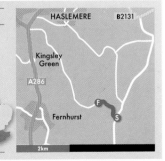

120 BARHATCH LANE

CRANLEIGH, SURREY

Statistically this is the hardest climb in the south-east, and the stats don't lie. If you're not having a good day on the bike, avoid this road like the plague, it takes no prisoners. The climb starts at the junction with Amlets Lane, passing first a 21% gradient sign then the Cranleigh Golf and Country Club; the incline is steady. You ride through a tunnel of trees that keeps the road shaded on even the brightest of days, up and up, but it's not yet the 21% advertised at the bottom. When will the steep stuff kick in you ask? Down a slight dip, past various houses and still it's manageable, the trepidation builds – steep, then easing, then steep – it's no killer yet but slowly and surely it's wearing the legs down. Pass a second 21% sign and here it is, the remorselessly tough top section. This has to be steeper than 21% – it must be 25% – you have to make it to the brow at the top and just hope you have a gear low enough.

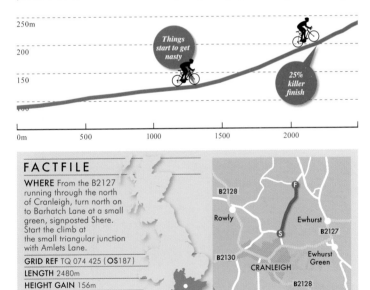

250m

200

150

100

0m   500   1000   1500   2000

Things start to get nasty

25% killer finish

FACTFILE

WHERE From the B2127 running through the north of Cranleigh, turn north on to Barhatch Lane at a small green, signposted Shere. Start the climb at the small triangular junction with Amlets Lane.

GRID REF TQ 074 425 (OS187)

LENGTH 2480m

HEIGHT GAIN 156m

APPROX CLIMB TIME 10mins

B2128

Rowly

Ewhurst

B2127

B2130

Ewhurst Green

CRANLEIGH

B2128

2km

RATING
5/10

121 DRAGON HILL ROAD

WOOLSTONE, OXFORDSHIRE

Dragon Hill Road has no earthly place here, climbing out of the Vale of the White Horse, it is as if it's been transported rock by rock from the Peak District. This little patch of isolated beauty with its narrow chalk-stained road is a real find, and to boot, seriously tough to climb. Essentially, it's a road to nowhere, a detour; you leave the B4507, ride the climb then loop back past the White Horse visitors car park to rejoin the same road. The climb starts as you leave the main road. Cross a rickety cattle grid and make your way up the tight road as it enters the beautiful, almost vertical, grassy banks. The gradient is at worst 1-in-6 and eases about halfway before reaching its steepest stretch after a 90-degree right-hand bend. There's little sign of the white horse – it is way above you – so keep one eye on the road and the other on the awesome view as you roll to a finish at a National Trust car park.

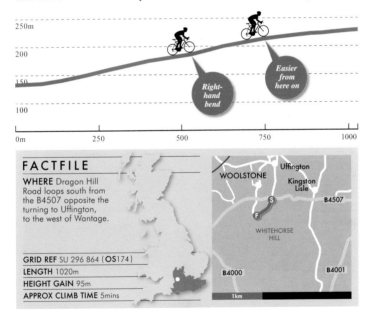

FACTFILE

WHERE Dragon Hill Road loops south from the B4507 opposite the turning to Uffington, to the west of Wantage.

GRID REF SU 296 864 (**OS**174)

LENGTH 1020m

HEIGHT GAIN 95m

APPROX CLIMB TIME 5mins

122 KINGSTON HILL

KINGSTON BLOUNT, OXFORDSHIRE

RATING 2/10

There are many roads that criss-cross the Chiltern ridge, in fact you could cycle all day, up and down, and not ride the same climb twice. True, none of them are real killers, there are no 33% gradients but a great climb doesn't always have to be steep. Start at the sign for the Kingston Blount Point to Point races, just before the gradient bites then really attack it. It's a short climb so try to ride it at maximum from start to finish, keep the legs spinning, keep on top of your gear and keep your effort high to power all the way through. The slope is gentle at first but as the daylight is replaced by the shadows of branches overhead things get gradually tougher. Meandering left then right then left, the higher slopes are worn and pitted making your task harder, but keep on top of things to finish just shy of the right turn sign next to a private footpath on the left.

FACTFILE

WHERE The road heads south from the B4009 from the village of Kingston Blount just south of Chinnor.

GRID REF SU 746 973 (OS165)

LENGTH 1165m

HEIGHT GAIN 99m

APPROX CLIMB TIME 5mins

KINGSTON BLOUNT

B4009

Aston Rowant

A40

M40

1km

123 DOWN LANE

VENTNOR, ISLE OF WIGHT

I'd had a tip-off that there were some super-steep hills in the town of Ventnor on the Isle of Wight so I went to check them out. I wasn't disappointed. The small town is packed with vicious little streets, and quite literally to top them all off is Down Lane. It's a silky smooth twisting narrow road that's almost 20% for its entirety and steeper still in the corners. Although a serious climb in itself, for a greater challenge you can ride all the way from the beach to the summit by combining these three excellent roads. Starting from the western end of the Esplanade, take the very short but perfectly formed 25% Bath Road, make a left at the top then right at the T-junction on to the A3055. The next left brings you on to the quite unique hairpins of Zig Zag Road that lead you to the junction with Ocean View Road. Turn right then follow round the corner taking your first right to start the final climb – Down Lane.

FACTFILE

WHERE Head north out of Ventnor on Ocean View Road the B3327. Through the hairpin bend it turns into Newport Road, take the next right turn, heading east and that's Down Lane.

GRID REF SZ 562 784 (OS196)

LENGTH 1375m

HEIGHT GAIN 98m

APPROX CLIMB TIME 6mins

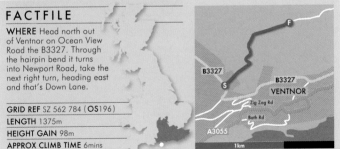

EAST

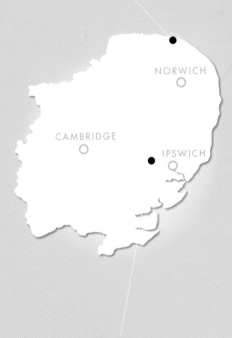

125 Beacon Hill

NORWICH
○

CAMBRIDGE
○

IPSWICH
● ○

124 Watson's Hill

WATSON'S HILL

SEMER, SUFFOLK

Before you skip the next two pages, yes there are climbs in the east of England – granted, the majority of it is a barren, flat wasteland, but if you look hard enough you'll find one. Let's start in Suffolk – here, nestled just above Hadleigh in a warren of roads is Watson's or Semer Hill. The surrounding area is surprisingly lumpy without a stretch of flat in sight and this hill is the hidden gem, the climb that the local clubs use to see which of the flatlanders can climb the best. It's a short, sharp effort. Begin in the hollow of the road next to the lamp-post marked with the number '2'. Head towards the house on the corner in front of you, the road bends left then climbs steeper at no less than the advertised 11% gradient. You'll not have much traffic to contend with apart from the local agricultural vehicles as you climb towards the final tough kick to the top that's marked by another lamp-post, this one marked with the number '1'.

FACTFILE

WHERE Travel north from Hadleigh on the A1141 then leave it to join the B1115 continuing north. Next take the second left to Semer and start the climb at the lamp-post marked '2'.

GRID REF TL 996 462 (**OS**155)

LENGTH 560m

HEIGHT GAIN 32m

APPROX CLIMB TIME 3mins

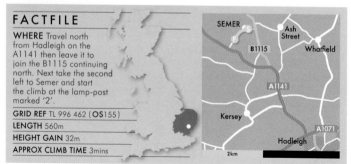

BEACON HILL

WEST RUNTON, NORFOLK

Norfolk isn't entirely flat, anyone who lives in Norwich will tell you that, but yes, most of it is – apart from a ridge that runs the length of the beautiful north coast. I have a particular affection for this part of the world as it's where I spent the majority of my childhood holidays and, although it's not hilly, it is fantastic cycling country. Of the handful of tiny climbs that scale the ridge, arguably the best is Bard Hill out of Salthouse, but for this book I've included the longer Beacon Hill. Leave the A149 in West Runton heading south on Sandy Lane to start the climb outside the golf club. The road rises steadily to a row of typical flint-clad cottages then ramps up a bit, it then eases and doesn't kick up again until you dip under the cover of trees. The now substantial gradient levels at a brief clearing then heads back under more trees for a final, slightly steeper, flourish to the brow at the highest point in the county.

FACTFILE

WHERE Leave the A149 in West Runton and follow the signs to the station. Head over the railway line and begin the climb at the turning before the first entrance to The Links golf club.

GRID REF TG 185 412 (**OS**133)

LENGTH 1250m

HEIGHT GAIN 68m

APPROX CLIMB TIME 6mins

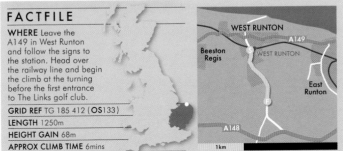

MIDLANDS

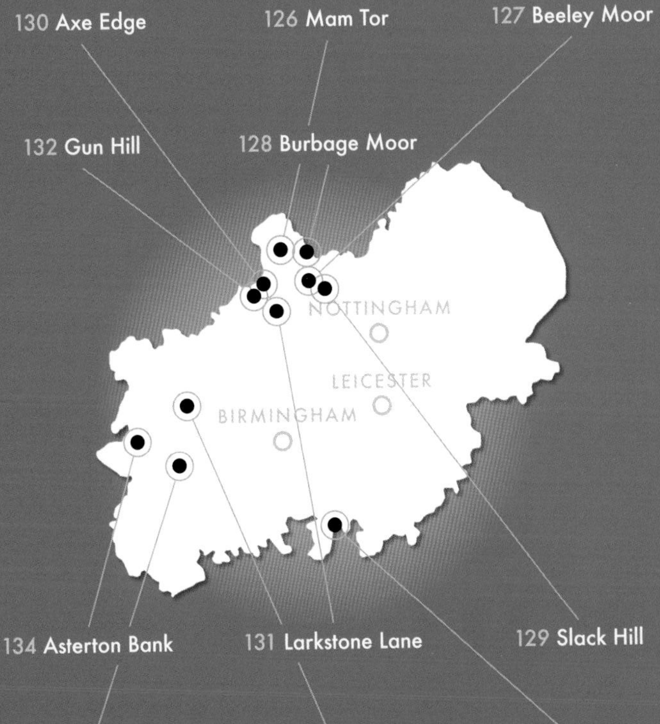

130 Axe Edge

126 Mam Tor

127 Beeley Moor

132 Gun Hill

128 Burbage Moor

NOTTINGHAM

LEICESTER

BIRMINGHAM

134 Asterton Bank

131 Larkstone Lane

129 Slack Hill

135 Clee Hill

133 The Wrekin

136 Edge Hill

126 MAM TOR

BARBER BOOTH, DERBYSHIRE

Mam Tor is a marvellous snaking road that climbs up out of Edale to Rushup Edge. It's tough, but a good few degrees kinder than the infamous Winnats Pass on the other side of the ridge. Beginning just outside the village of Barber Booth, the gradient hits 1-in-6 straight away as you cross a small bridge, but only for a short distance before easing off. Following the first left bend it's easier still but this doesn't last long; more tough stuff is on its way. Mam Tor, which translated means 'Heights of the Mother', looms way above, watching you as the road gets steeper, weaving left and right like water flowing between rocks in a stream. As you enter the last few bends, it appears as if a giant blanket of green felt has been laid over the land smoothing all the rocks and bumps. Keep pushing through this surreal Tellytubbies-like scenery to finish where the road cuts its way through the gap in the ridge.

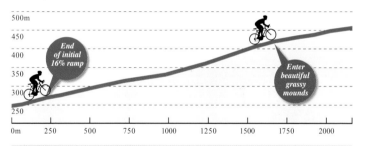

500m
450
400 — End of initial 16% ramp
350
300 — Enter beautiful grassy mounds
250

0m   250   500   750   1000   1250   1500   1750   2000

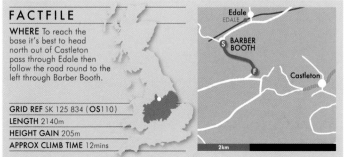

FACTFILE

WHERE To reach the base it's best to head north out of Castleton pass through Edale then follow the road round to the left through Barber Booth.

GRID REF SK 125 834 (**OS**110)

LENGTH 2140m

HEIGHT GAIN 205m

APPROX CLIMB TIME 12mins

Edale
EDALE
BARBER BOOTH
Castleton
2km

127 BEELEY MOOR

BEELEY, DERBYSHIRE

Beeley Lane up to Beeley Moor is a frequently used hill climb course, not quite steep enough for the pure climbers but a great road nonetheless. Start from the T-junction outside the Devonshire Arms in the centre of the village. The hardest slopes are in the first third so you can put some extra effort in here safe in the knowledge that things will get easier further up. Following a noticeable increase in gradient there's a brief levelling and from here on it's just a degree gentler. You can either take this as the signal to relax a little, or click down a gear and keep pushing as the road meanders in and out of the cover of the woods. Exiting the trees for a final time, push through the last bend that takes you on to the exposed moor. The gradient continues to ebb away but at the same time your exposure to the elements increases, ensuring the long ride to the brow is an effort all the way.

FACTFILE

WHERE If you're heading north on the A6, leave this road at the turning to Rowsley and join the B6012. Then turn right into Beeley and follow the road round to the right, past the Devonshire Arms pub.

GRID REF SK 296 672 (OS119)

LENGTH 3870m

HEIGHT GAIN 225m

APPROX CLIMB TIME 13mins

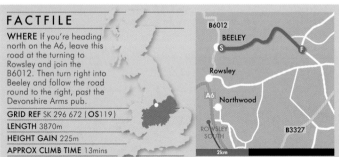

128 BURBAGE MOOR

HATHERSAGE, DERBYSHIRE

Linking Derbyshire and Yorkshire, the climb out of Hathersage isn't to be underestimated. To begin the climb make your way south out of Hathersage on the A6187 then take a left turn on to School Lane. The road levels outside St Michael's Primary School, and you start the climb proper from here. Up and round to the right past the Scotsmans Pack pub, through the houses and as you leave the last one behind, it gets harder as it begins to bend left. After backing off a pinch, the road next makes its way round to the right and ramps up steeper and steeper towards a left-hand bend. Here the hard climbing ends for a while and up ahead you see the exposed rock face, which on any day will be dotted with brightly clad climbers. Ride up to the base, level out, then bank right into the finale. A solid slog, punctuated only by a couple of sets of rumble strips, the second set coming just before the peak of the road as the gradient disappears to level out and finish.

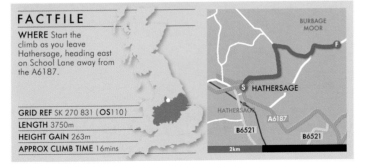

FACTFILE

WHERE Start the climb as you leave Hathersage, heading east on School Lane away from the A6187.

GRID REF SK 270 831 (**OS**110)

LENGTH 3750m

HEIGHT GAIN 263m

APPROX CLIMB TIME 16mins

129 SLACK HILL

KELSTEDGE, DERBYSHIRE

I've never had a good time on this road – I hate it, I hate it so much, which is the very reason why I had to include it – it is such an unforgiving beast. The first time I came across its cruel slopes was on a youth hostelling weekend many years ago, but that time I rode down it. The aim was to see who could achieve the highest speed; I chickened out at 57 mph, and to this day I still think that's the fastest I've ever been on two wheels. But to climb Slack Hill is just evil; if bikes had been around in medieval times people would have been forced to ride up it as a form of torture. Approaching from Kelstedge you're faced with the sight of the huge arc of 14% tarmac heading skywards, take all the momentum you can to the base and begin to suffer. There are no corners, no deviation, just struggling. Of course the torment does come to an end – over the brow just past the turning to Beeley. Now, how fast do you dare ride down it?

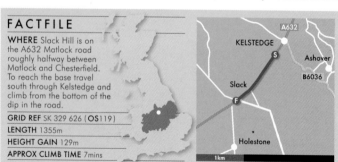

FACTFILE

WHERE Slack Hill is on the A632 Matlock road roughly halfway between Matlock and Chesterfield. To reach the base travel south through Kelstedge and climb from the bottom of the dip in the road.

GRID REF SK 329 626 (OS119)

LENGTH 1355m

HEIGHT GAIN 129m

APPROX CLIMB TIME 7mins

MIDLANDS

130 AXE EDGE

Not quite as harsh as its name suggests, Axe Edge is nonetheless a solid climb which can be a real morale breaker in the wrong conditions. The ascent begins somewhere in the busy centre of Buxton but I chose to measure my distance from the final set of traffic lights at the junction with the B5059. Rising gently away from town, a little steeper past a garage and the junctions leading to Macclesfield, you are soon free of habitation and heading towards the Edge. The whole climb is now lined out in front of you – a constant, exposed gradient stretching up and round the gritstone mound. As you enter the Peak District National Park choose your gear and settle into a comfortable rhythm to drive you along the smooth but attritional surface. Reaching a fake summit, the road is lined with a chequered Armco barrier, you then drop a little, so shift up and power to the second brow and true finish.

FACTFILE

WHERE The base of this road lies in the centre of Buxton but to avoid traffic lights, I measured my distance from the last set, at the junction with the B5059, you then simply head south-east on the A53 to the top.

GRID REF SK 034 694 (OS119)

LENGTH 3830m

HEIGHT GAIN 162m

APPROX CLIMB TIME 14mins

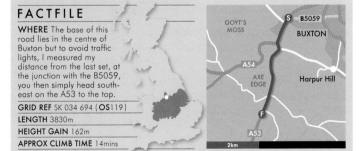

RATING
6/10

131 LARKSTONE LANE

GRINDON, STAFFORDSHIRE

In a quiet corner of the Peak District, far from the madding crowds surrounding Matlock and Buxton, lies the Manifold Valley. Of the number of ways in and out of the gorge, Larkstone Lane is the toughest. Riding from Grindon, there is a very nasty rough descent so take care. Cross a small stone bridge then follow the road as it bends right climbing gently towards the initial hairpin. Here's where the hard work begins – 25% at its apex it delivers you into a gruelling 20% stretch before doubling back on itself at the next horribly steep corner. The road, now edged with the typical drystone wall, climbs gently for a while before ramping up again as the surface slowly deteriorates. Before long you're left with just a few inches of clean tarmac either side of the grass and rubble that cover the crown, and then you dip down before the final rise to the summit at the junction with Ashbourne Lane.

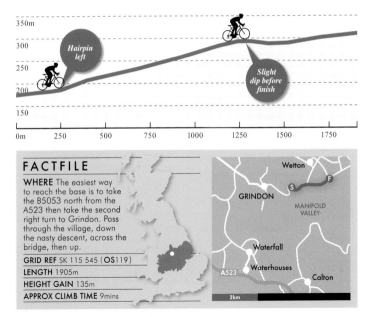

FACTFILE

WHERE The easiest way to reach the base is to take the B5053 north from the A523 then take the second right turn to Grindon. Pass through the village, down the nasty descent, across the bridge, then up.

GRID REF SK 115 545 (OS119)

LENGTH 1905m

HEIGHT GAIN 135m

APPROX CLIMB TIME 9mins

132 GUN HILL

RATING 5/10

Start the climb of Gun Hill outside the Lazy Trout in the village of Meerbrook. The slope is gentle at first as you move away from the scattered houses, bending slightly left then later right, heading into a cover of trees. After this kink, the gradient starts to bite and it becomes a completely different climb. It's steep now and the surface is rough and broken. This double whammy of hindrances will seriously slow your pace. Exiting the shade of the trees the road begins to step its way towards the exposed summit, first hard, then easing, then hard, each step up tougher than the one before and delivering you to a large sweeping right-hand bend. This marks the beginning of the end of the steep stuff. In a race this is where the strong men would make it hurt, consolidating any advantage they have over those distanced on the lower slopes – change down and build your momentum to get you to the finish at the brow.

FACTFILE

WHERE Head north out of Leek on the A53 then take the left turning to Meerbrook. Ride past the Tittesworth Reservoir and start the climb outside the Lazy Trout Public House.

GRID REF SJ 967 609 (**OS**118)	
LENGTH 2380m	
HEIGHT GAIN 151m	
APPROX CLIMB TIME 11mins	

Meerbrook

Blackshaw Moor

A523

A53

Rudyard

LEEK

2km

133 THE WREKIN

WELLINGTON, SHROPSHIRE

West of Telford lies the Wrekin, a lone giant protruding from the landscape. Such is its dominance on the horizon that it holds a special place in local folklore. Not the longest or hardest climb in the land, it is nevertheless the most significant in this corner of England and a serious challenge. There are two ways up and over, neither of which takes you to the top – that is reached only by foot. To tackle the climb from the north, leave the Wrekin car park and climb gently through the woods at the base of a large rock face. The surface through a dense tunnel of trees is rough and bumpy as you wind your way, climbing steeper as you approach the exit of the forest. With the Wrekin on your right the road flattens and the surface improves, passing farmhouses and the road climbs hard again. Bending right, then left, the last push will have your legs burning as you reach the top and roll down into Little Wenlock.

FACTFILE

WHERE To ride the Wrekin leave Telford on the B5061 and follow the road under the M54. Pass Cluddley then at the junction at the Wrekin car park you start to climb.

GRID REF SJ 641 078 (**OS**127)

LENGTH 1630m

HEIGHT GAIN 102m

APPROX CLIMB TIME 7mins

RATING

10/10

134 ASTERTON BANK

ASTERTON, SHROPSHIRE

On the eastern edge of the Long Mynd lies the infamous Asterton Bank, although it is also known by many other names, there are none that I can print here. Without being too hysterical, this climb is nothing more than a joyless straight line of pain. Start opposite the old red telephone box, past the numerous warning signs, across the cattle grid then bend slightly left. You're now face to face with the vicious 25% corner, which delivers you on to the cruel slopes that cling to the side of the sheer bank. The surface, just wide enough for a single car is smooth at the edges but little more than gravel and moss in the centre. It never relents, never lets up until you reach the bend in the shadow of a rocky outcrop, you've still a fair bit of climbing to reach the top, but not as hard now. You will, however, be able to reacquaint your backside with the saddle for the final push to summit on the approach to the gliding club.

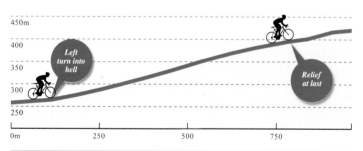

450m
400
350
300
250

Left turn into hell

Relief at last

0m   250   500   750

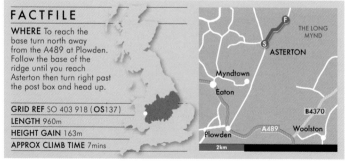

FACTFILE

WHERE To reach the base turn north away from the A489 at Plowden. Follow the base of the ridge until you reach Asterton then turn right past the post box and head up.

GRID REF SO 403 918 (OS137)

LENGTH 960m

HEIGHT GAIN 163m

APPROX CLIMB TIME 7mins

THE LONG MYND
ASTERTON
Myndtown
Eaton
B4370
Plowden   A489   Woolston
2km

135 CLEE HILL

The solitary Clee Hill sits just outside Ludlow, an isolated peak at the bottom end of the Shropshire hills topped with a science fiction-like radar station. Beginning at the T-junction opposite the Angel Bank garage, the surface on the early slopes is a mess; there are holes within holes and patches upon patches, evidence of years of neglect and sub-standard repairs. It's fairly steep up to a group of houses where there's a little respite then it's hard again to a cattle grid. The climb next eases and dips slightly to the base of the final push to the summit, and the 'golf ball' radar that sits on the horizon. Not too steep but still a challenge up to a plateau and a right-hand bend. Here you're greeted with a faded 'no entry' sign, I kept riding through the decaying abandoned buildings, past the second 'no entry' sign until I reached a third sign at the gates of the station compound where I finally got the message and turned back.

FACTFILE

WHERE Travelling east from Ludlow on the A4117 the road climbs up towards the village of Cleehill. The climb starts at the left turn opposite the Angel Bank garage on Dhustone Lane.

GRID REF SO 597 776 (OS137)

LENGTH 3350m

HEIGHT GAIN 185m

APPROX CLIMB TIME 14mins

136 EDGE HILL

Edge Hill dominates the skyline to the north-west of Banbury, a raised peninsula jutting up from the northern edge of the Cotswolds. Of the number of ways up the ridge I've chosen the B4086 through Knowle Wood. Not as tough or as steep as the A422 (Sun Rising Hill) to its west, but a far nicer ride than the very busy A-road. Start the climb at the junction with Gosport Lane and head up towards the ridge. You've a gentle prelude as the road bends smoothly upwards round to the right. Through the corner your legs will be tested as the road straightens and heads up towards the woods. Once into the protection of the trees, the gradient starts to bite. The road is wide and well surfaced and although never drastically steep it's certainly a slog and, if anything, gets that little bit steeper as you approach the summit, which arrives at the T-junction. Now you can head on into the Cotswolds.

FACTFILE

WHERE Edge Hill lies just south of the M40 north of Banbury. Follow the B4086 south-east from Kineton and start the climb at the junction with Gosport Lane.

GRID REF SP 380 482 (**OS**151)

LENGTH 1060m

HEIGHT GAIN 105m

APPROX CLIMB TIME 5mins

YORKSHIRE

142 Turf Moor

145 Trapping Hill

149 Caper Hill

144 Greets Moss

146 Nought Bank Road

147 Sleights Moor

143 Bowland Knotts

150 Egton High Moor

YORK

LEEDS

SHEFFIELD

140 Thwaites Brow

141 Hainworth Lane

137 Ewden Bank

148 Blakey Bank

139 Mytholm Steeps

138 Cragg Vale

151 Hanging Grimston

137 EWDEN BANK

STOCKSBRIDGE, SOUTH YORKSHIRE

Take a map of the area between Sheffield and the High Peak, throw a dart at it, and you'll hit a hill. Collectively known as the Strines, it's packed with a myriad of steep climbs. If you want a really tough ride take Mortimer Road from the A57 and ride north until you meet the A616. You'll tackle many ascents on its course and the best is saved till last, the wicked Ewden Bank. With your legs well softened up, pass across the old bridge over the beck, and bend right into a very steep ramp leading you to a 25% left-hand bend. Brutally steep on the inside, scarred by the undercarriages of vehicles it leads you into more punishing gradient that lasts until you leave the cover of trees. Past some farm buildings, the slope backs off a little before slowly building up again to the right-hand bend into the last very hard ramp to the finish. Grind your way up to the sweeping left-hand bend, in front the road disappears over the brow and you finish.

FACTFILE

WHERE Ewden Bank lies on Mortimer Road linking the A616 and the A57. I'd recommend riding all the way north from the A57, it's a tough route up and down all the way. You start the climb after crossing Ewden beck.

GRID REF SK 239 975 (**OS**110)

LENGTH 1035m

HEIGHT GAIN 107m

APPROX CLIMB TIME 7mins

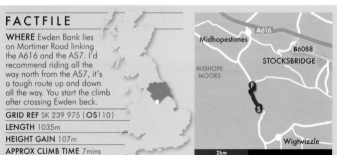

138 CRAGG VALE

Cragg Vale isn't the toughest climb, however it is the longest continuous uphill gradient in England, and there's a sign at the base that proudly boasts this fact. Leaving Mytholmroyd, start the climb as the road crosses Cragg Brook. The slope is very gentle at first, then kicks up slightly as you enter Cragg Vale itself. The further you progress through the village, the steeper it gets and the hardest part of the climb comes as you finally escape the protection of the houses. The gradient eases back and all is good, however, having left the shelter of buildings and trees you're now left exposed to the full force of any wind. The road continues straight with a slight right–left dog-leg towards its peak, and as you wind up your sprint for the large sign on the left, the horizon appears to shimmer. It's not a mirage, though, but the reservoir butting right up to the edge of the road, following you to the finish at the T-junction.

FACTFILE

WHERE The base of Cragg Vale lies in Mytholmroyd. Leave the A646 in the centre of the town and head south on the B6138. Ride over the river, under the railway bridge then follow the road to the right.

GRID REF SD 975 180 (**OS**104)

LENGTH 9160m

HEIGHT GAIN 286m

APPROX CLIMB TIME 28mins

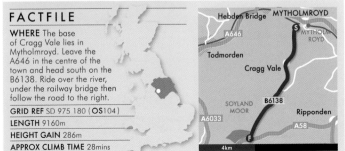

RATING
10/10

139 MYTHOLM STEEPS

HEBDEN BRIDGE, WEST YORKSHIRE

This road goes by many names: the Mytholm Steeps, Rawtenstall Bank and Blackshaw Head, but one thing is certain – it's a hellishly tough climb. Start from the junction with the A646, stick it in (and this is very important) your second lowest gear and head off, don't under any circumstances engage your largest sprocket, not yet. Bank right round the church then left, left, straight, right and left again. The road twists its path up through the houses, hairpin bend after hairpin bend until you exit the buildings to climb a steep stretch that levels next to a small passing place. Now you engage that gear you've held in reserve, and oh yes you'll need it as you climb a remorseless, leg-breaking rise up to a wicked left-hand bend. Next there's an easier stretch to the final hairpin and you're through the worst of it. Now on the moor, you've just the gentle journey to the top to finish at the junction in Blackshaw Head.

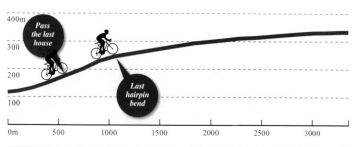

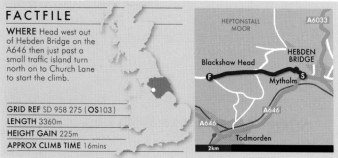

FACTFILE

WHERE Head west out of Hebden Bridge on the A646 then just past a small traffic island turn north on to Church Lane to start the climb.

GRID REF SD 958 275 (OS103)

LENGTH 3360m

HEIGHT GAIN 225m

APPROX CLIMB TIME 16mins

140 THWAITES BROW

The best cobbled climb this side of Flanders? Maybe. This unforgiving, super-rugged road is such a fantastic hill to ride and has humble beginnings in an industrial estate. In fact, there's nothing picturesque about Thwaites Brow at all, but forget your surroundings, just focus on those stones. Hard from the get-go, the cobbles come at you from every conceivable angle with an almost total lack of uniformity. The road bends round to the right and then left into a set of savage zigzag bends and then straight away into another set – these, even more merciless than the first. Exit the bends on the jarring surface towards some houses, bank left, steep right then left to leave the cobbles and continue on tarmac. Don't for one second think it's going to get easier, because the next stretch up to the Druid Arms is the steepest of all, and you're still left with a couple of lumps before you finally peak at the crossroads past Moss Car Road.

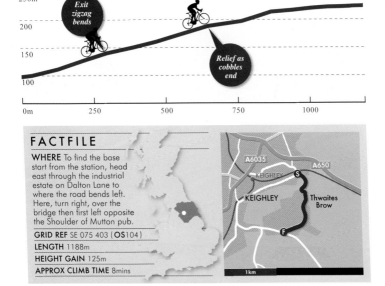

FACTFILE

WHERE To find the base start from the station, head east through the industrial estate on Dalton Lane to where the road bends left. Here, turn right, over the bridge then first left opposite the Shoulder of Mutton pub.

GRID REF SE 075 403 (**OS**104)

LENGTH 1188m

HEIGHT GAIN 125m

APPROX CLIMB TIME 8mins

141 HAINWORTH LANE

KEIGHLEY, WEST YORKSHIRE

Hainworth Lane may be famous for its cobbles but there's much more to it than that. It's a beast of a climb when ridden from base to summit and packs in a little bit of everything. Leaving the A629 you see the 20% warning sign, the smooth road bends right then left, very steep over the bridge before entering a canyon of tall houses. You reach the cobbles after the junction with Hainworth Wood Road, and, although far more uniform than Thwaites Brow or the Shibden Wall, these are still proper, solid, northern cobbles. About halfway up there's a nasty left-hand corner that will have you stretching every single sinew in your legs, but after this it calms down up to the final very hard right-hand bend that returns you to tarmac. As the constant bouncing disappears, it's as if the turbo kicks in – you'll fly through the village and on to a final steep lip before finishing just shy of the junction.

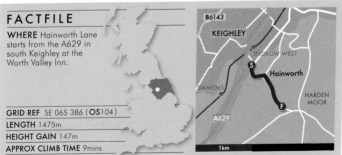

FACTFILE

WHERE Hainworth Lane starts from the A629 in south Keighley at the Worth Valley Inn.

GRID REF SE 065 386 (OS104)

LENGTH 1475m

HEIGHT GAIN 147m

APPROX CLIMB TIME 9mins

B6143

KEIGHLEY

INGROW WEST

S Hainworth

DAMEMS

HARDEN MOOR

F

A629

1km

142 TURF MOOR

FEETHAM, YORKSHIRE DALES

RATING
6/10

Leave Feetham in Swaledale and head straight up a nasty 17% stretch into a cover of trees. The surface is pitted and continues hard until you bend left and cross a cattle grid. Lessening slightly, the tarmac is now broken and scarred from a series of sub-standard repairs. Ahead you will see a lone tree on the left, which marks the end of the opening section. The stiff climb out of Feetham is behind you, but you are still far from the summit on Turf Moor. Next you roll for a while, sweeping down a couple of short 16% drops, the first over a bridge but the second leading you to a formidable double obstacle. Your challenge is to cross a ford, then, with wet tyres, a cattle grid. However, if you are at all unsure, there is a footbridge you can use to avoid the ford. Now you'll quickly need to build momentum to ride the cattle grid and launch straight up into two tight bends and a final section of 16% before rolling to the top.

FACTFILE

WHERE Start the climb from the small village of Feetham on the B6270 in Swaledale.

GRID REF NY 993 014 (OS98)
LENGTH 3350m
HEIGHT GAIN 190m
APPROX CLIMB TIME 14mins

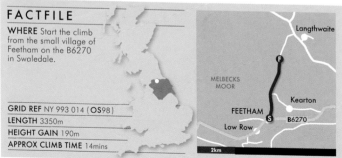

RATING 5/10

143 BOWLAND KNOTTS

KEASDEN, NORTH YORKSHIRE

An epic route across a barren windswept moor, the course up to Bowland Knotts stutters a bit to get going but once in its stride it's just a brilliant road. I'm taking the start from the bridge over Wenning Beck. It's gentle at first and you roll up and down for a while before heading into a long, straight, demanding stretch. It eases slightly past some buildings, then climbs again heading for the summit on the ridge. As the top came into view I began to think, is that it? I wanted much more, and thankfully over this brow more is what I got, a lot more. Here you're faced with the true nature of the beast, as in front of you the road snakes onwards and upwards across the featureless landscape. It's never too steep, but it's slow progress to the top. Crossing the tiny Cowsen Gill Bridge you're led to another brow, but still not the top. This road goes on and on, eventually to finish across a cattle grid surrounded by the huge stone Knotts.

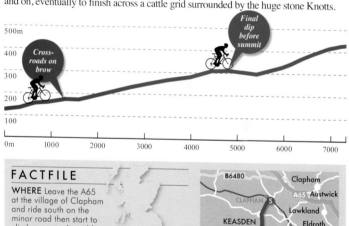

FACTFILE

WHERE Leave the A65 at the village of Clapham and ride south on the minor road then start to climb once you've ridden under the railway bridge and over the river.

GRID REF SD 726 606 (OS98)

LENGTH 7340m

HEIGHT GAIN 299m

APPROX CLIMB TIME 21mins

144 GREETS MOSS

GRINTON, YORKSHIRE DALES

Of the two ways out of Grinton that link Swaledale with Wensleydale, the best climb is via the barren Greets Moss. Both climbs have the same origin in the centre of the village. You climb steeply through the houses and, leaving the last building behind you, must then traverse probably the steepest cattle grid I've ever come across. It is always awkward to cross them slowly and here nigh on impossible to build sufficient speed to take you comfortably over the gaping bars. Once over this obstacle the road is still steep but does ease as you reach a junction. Turn right here and head straight into more 16% climbing through a snaking S-bend. It's a long way to the top after this – the decent surface undulates, rolls left and right, throws in another short stretch of 16% and drops a little as it picks its way up and over the moor to deliver you to the peak just past a second – this time more sensible – cattle grid.

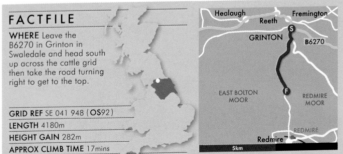

FACTFILE

WHERE Leave the B6270 in Grinton in Swaledale and head south up across the cattle grid then take the road turning right to get to the top.

GRID REF SE 041 948 (**OS**92)	
LENGTH 4180m	
HEIGHT GAIN 282m	
APPROX CLIMB TIME 17mins	

145 TRAPPING HILL

LOFTHOUSE, NIDDERDALE

Deep in the heart of sleepy Nidderdale, to the east of the Yorkshire Dales lies the small village of Lofthouse and rising from its centre is the brilliant Trapping Hill. You always know you're in for some fun every time you see the 'unsuitable for heavy goods vehicles and buses' sign – it's a badge of honour that really tough hills are always proud to display. Leaving the main road you bank steep past The Crown Hotel to level slightly in the centre of the village, pass the stone cross then climb steeper away from the houses. Up and up, bending right, the landscape is open but soon large, high stone walls frame the road and you bend left up towards a lone, giant tree. Next, you reach a seriously steep bend but once free of this, and for the first time since you left the village, the climbing eases. You've now a long plateau and some very slight gradient before the draining final push to the summit across a cattle grid.

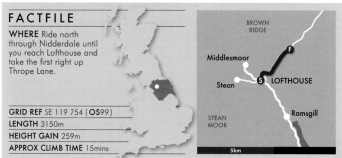

FACTFILE

WHERE Ride north through Nidderdale until you reach Lofthouse and take the first right up Thrope Lane.

GRID REF SE 119 754 (OS99)

LENGTH 3150m

HEIGHT GAIN 259m

APPROX CLIMB TIME 15mins

BROWN RIDGE

Middlesmoor

Stean

STEAN MOOR

F

S LOFTHOUSE

Ramsgill

5km

146 NOUGHT BANK ROAD

There are four great climbs that leave Pateley Bridge and one of them, Greenhow Hill, made it into the first *100 Greatest Cycling Climbs* (Hill No. 52). Nought Bank Road, is neither as long nor does it reach the same altitude as Greenhow but it is steeper, a lot steeper. A short way out of Pateley Bridge, across a bridge the road bends right then straight away left into a corner so steep you'll be forced to the wrong side of the road, so take care. The slope then relaxes a little before plunging you back into snaking bend after snaking bend, getting steeper through each turn and incrementally directing you round to the right towards Yorke's Folly. The push to the summit is a stunning stretch of road framed by the exposed rocks, but what appears for all the world to be the top is nothing more than a long, levelled left-hand bend. You have to continue, and it's still steep, the road bisects a stone wall then continues to a slight right bend where it levels out.

FACTFILE

WHERE Head west out of Pateley Bridge on the B6265 then opposite the Royal Oak pub turn left on to Bridgehouse Gate. Begin the climb over a small bridge at the corner, where the road becomes Naught Bank Road.

GRID REF SE 160 628 (OS99)

LENGTH 2350m

HEIGHT GAIN 207m

APPROX CLIMB TIME 12mins

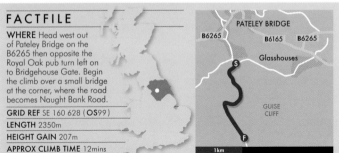

PATELEY BRIDGE

B6265   B6165   B6265

Glasshouses

S

GUISE CLIFF

F

1km

GROSMONT, NORTH YORK MOORS

There's a multitude of wickedly steep roads that take you out of the small villages in the labyrinth of valleys of the North York Moors. The climb up to Sleights Moor starts as you enter Grosmont. Ride under the rail bridge, bend round to the left and up into the village. It's not terribly tough until you cross more railway lines but then it really starts to hurt, steep through the houses, bending slightly right and left up to the point where the road splits. Take the right fork past the 33% sign – yes 33% – and then the road bends left then sharp right past another 33% sign. However, I'm somewhat doubtful of its claim, yes it's steep, but 1-in-3? I don't think so. The hard stuff is soon behind you; you've a substantial respite before it toughens up again to the cattle grid. Across the grid and the scenery changes, you're now on open moor and the slope is almost non-existent, but it's still a long way to the finish next to two large gates on the right.

FACTFILE

WHERE Ride into Grosmont heading south east from Egton and start the climb as you pass under the railway bridge. Once through the village take the right fork past the 33% sign.

GRID REF NZ 856 038 (**OS**94)

LENGTH 3320m

HEIGHT GAIN 250m

APPROX CLIMB TIME 13mins

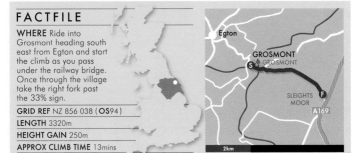

148 BLAKEY BANK

CHURCH HOUSES, NORTH YORK MOORS

They just don't do flat in the North York Moors, there isn't an inch of it, anywhere, so when a hill has its own signposts then you know it must be something special. Your legs will be sore no matter how you reach the base, unless you drive, because, like I said, it's all up and down, with the majority of it very, very, steep. Riding out of Church Houses you head up and over a hump to begin the climb across a stream on the weathered and worn early slopes. It's hard straight away up to a junction on the right and a 20% sign, steep again up to a cattle grid, then levelling; this is your last chance to really take a breather before plunging back into the remainder of the climb. It's a real beast, although not totally remorseless, following each brutal 20% stretch it takes pity on its prey and backs off slightly, just enough for you to take a drink, but then it's back on it, right the way to the point where the road ends at the top.

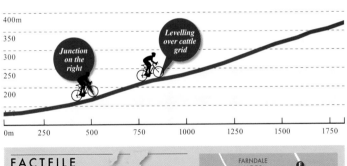

Junction on the right

Levelling over cattle grid

FACTFILE

WHERE Leave the tiny village of Church Houses heading north on Red Way. Ride up and over a small bump past a wood on the left then begin the climb at the small bridge as the road becomes Long Lane.

GRID REF SE 683 989 (**OS**94)

LENGTH 1860m

HEIGHT GAIN 232m

APPROX CLIMB TIME 12mins

FARNDALE MOOR

CHURCH HOUSES

Low Mill

2km

149 CAPER HILL

GLAISDALE, NORTH YORK MOORS

How do you choose one hill over another in a region where they all make you hurt and wheeze? What does a hill have to do to stand out more than its neighbour? In the case of Caper Hill it's simple, they didn't fuss about with loads of corners, they just built the road straight up from bottom to top: unrelenting in its gradient, and undeviating in its direction. You start from a small triangle of roads, the rusting signpost leaning over and pointing towards Rosedale. The lower slopes are the hardest, 25% on a very abrasive surface, all the way to a cattle grid – now a slight left then right, the only kink in this straight line of pain. The road disappears over the horizon, but each time you reach a brow, another one presents itself until you see the back of a warning sign slowly come into view. Only then do you know you're closing in on the summit – eke your way up, pass the sign and slump to a halt at the T-junction.

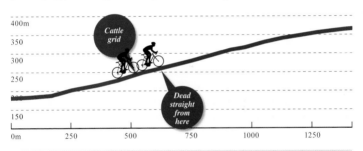

FACTFILE

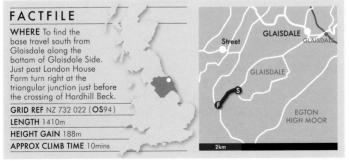

WHERE To find the base travel south from Glaisdale along the bottom of Glaisdale Side. Just past London House Farm turn right at the triangular junction just before the crossing of Hardhill Beck.

GRID REF NZ 732 022 (**OS**94)

LENGTH 1410m

HEIGHT GAIN 188m

APPROX CLIMB TIME 10mins

150 EGTON HIGH MOOR

EGTON BRIDGE, NORTH YORK MOORS

So frequent are the 33% gradient signs dotted around the North York Moors that it leads you to think there must have been a special offer on when the council placed the order. Start from the ford at the base, pass the warning sign and ride into some stiff, but no greater than, 17% climbing. It levels then you're into more of the same, and then steeper as you approach a group of houses. Here you enter the twin savage corners that have earned the 33% moniker. However, in my opinion they are, at worst, only 25%. Although a true brute, this is no Rosedale Chimney! Steepest through the second and continuing very tough it eases past more houses before delivering you into a long, wearing slog that ramps up in stages towards the open moor. Across a cattle grid and the steep climbing is over but it's still a long way to the top. Ride on and on across the open moor, the road only rising gently, but you'll still feel it in the legs all the way to the point where it levels.

FACTFILE

WHERE From the bridge over the River Esk in Egton Bridge ride up to a junction where the main road bends left past a 20% sign. Don't take this, head straight on signposted Rosedale, then begin after the ford.

GRID REF NZ 750 007 (OS94)

LENGTH 6750m

HEIGHT GAIN 279m

APPROX CLIMB TIME 19mins

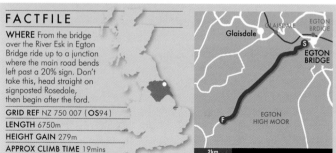

151 HANGING GRIMSTON

KIRBY UNDERDALE, EAST RIDING OF YORKSHIRE

If there's a climb in Britain with a more sinister name, I've yet to find it, and this beast of a road more than lives up to its unpleasant title. Sandwiched between the A64 and A166 in the Yorkshire Wolds, the ascent begins across a small stream just outside Kirby Underdale. It is immediately steep up a wonderfully smooth, dead straight, strength-sapping rise. This is followed by a gentle stretch but the nice surface soon turns nasty as you approach some farm buildings. Next you'll reach the first of two gates that bookend the middle section of the road as it bisects an empty grassy field. The gradient increases as you cross the field up to the second gate, then through this the climbing really kicks in. You begin a tough stretch of 1-in-6 on a now dreadfully pitted and deteriorating road and the climb remains steep and relentlessly rough until you reach the brow past the last tree on your left.

FACTFILE

WHERE Make your way through the village of Kirby Underdale, follow the road out, straight on and round to the left. Next you reach the right turn, signposted Hanging Grimston, head down and start across the stream.

GRID REF SE 800 607 (OS106)

LENGTH 1620m

HEIGHT GAIN 150m

APPROX CLIMB TIME 8mins

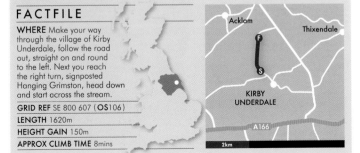

THE PAIN CAVE

I'm two-thirds through a hill climb and I've turned myself inside out, pushed myself to the limit. My arms and legs are buckling, my vision is blurred and my lungs burn as if I'm breathing fire. I've given almost all I have to give but still, still, I've only just reached the entrance. The adrenalin and nervous energy that propelled me from the start line are now just distant memory. I stand shattered, staring into the pitch black, dare I push further, dare I enter the Pain Cave.

All human instinct tells me to turn round, to keep out, I've gone far enough, but this is a race, a hill climb, and I must penetrate the darkness. I have to cross the barrier between tolerable discomfort and all out self torture. It's the only way to show what I'm made of, to do justice to the months of training, the commitment and the sacrifice. The question is posed, can I go on? In an event where half a second can cover five places, to hesitate is to lose, the answer must be instant. I must take my first step into the world where physical pain is no longer relevant; the battle is no longer with the body but now with the mind.

It's in this instant that I somehow instinctively flash to a scene from David Lynch's adaptation of Frank Herbert's Sci-Fi epic *Dune*. The principal character is to be observed, he sits in a dark room, nervous, and is obliged to place his hand inside a small metal box. Once out of his sight, a Bene Gesserit Sister holds a poison jab to his throat. Simply, if during the test he withdraws his hand, he dies.

"What's inside the box?" he asks.
"Pain," comes the simple answer.

The test begins and his hand starts to itch, the itching turns to burning, heat upon heat, the skin crisps and the flesh bubbles. He must focus; his ability to cope with pain is being pushed to the limit. He recalls a passage his mother taught him as a child and recites to himself...

"I must not fear. Fear is the mind-killer. Fear is the little-death that brings total obliteration. I will face my fear. I will permit it to pass over me and through me. And when it has gone past I will turn the inner eye to see its path. Where the fear has gone there will be nothing. Only I will remain."

In this alternate universe the test is designed to determine whether he is human or animal. A human's awareness is powerful enough to control its instincts; it can fight its urges, suppress them and leave its hand inside the box. When he removes his hand it's unharmed, the burning was an illusion, pain by nerve induction. A human can resist any pain, override the signals, whereas an animal cannot. A human can ride into the Pain Cave and survive; a human can ride into the Pain Cave and thrive. As we enter our box, our discomfort appears all too real but we cannot be afraid of it. Is it really pain? Pain is the loss of a loved one, having a limb severed in an accident. We must treat the pain we endure during a hill climb as an annoyance at worst. We must learn to embrace it, to, dare I say, enjoy it. If we can, then each time we return we can go deeper, further inside. If we can train ourselves to glide mentally through, to isolate our body from the mind whilst all hell unfolds around us we will become the riders we were born to be. Only when we trust our body to perform against its will, can we realise our true potential, then we will cease to fear and learn to love the Pain Cave.

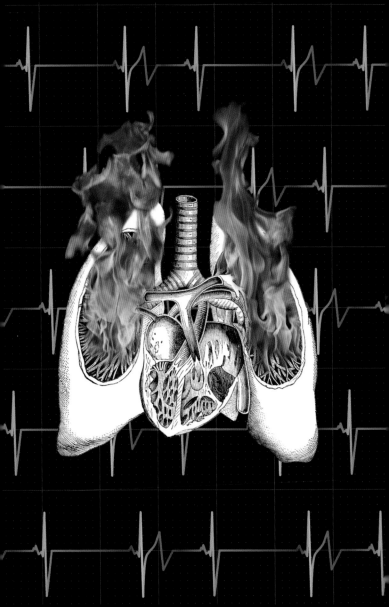

NORTH-EAST

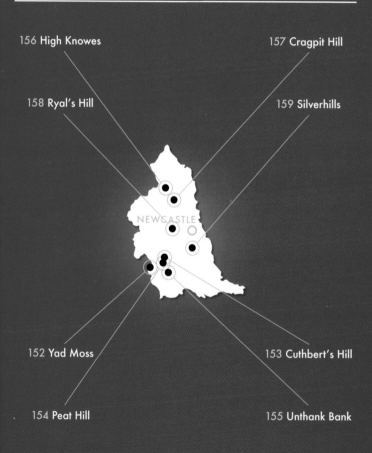

156 High Knowes

157 Cragpit Hill

158 Ryal's Hill

159 Silverhills

NEWCASTLE

152 Yad Moss

153 Cuthbert's Hill

154 Peat Hill

155 Unthank Bank

152 YAD MOSS

FOREST-IN-TEESDALE, COUNTY DURHAM

RATING 4/10

Although not quite Sir Ranulph Fiennes territory, it certainly feels like an adventure climbing up to and crossing the barren Yad Moss. Ride out from Middleton-in-Teesdale, roll up and down for a while then start the climb proper at the Forest-in-Teesdale sign. I haven't chosen many climbs that you can start in the big ring, but this is one. The gradient is very gentle at first so pick up speed and keep the large gear spinning for as long as you can. At the point where the road ramps up away from the last of the trees and past a couple of houses, I had to give in and change down, but when the course bent right and eased I engaged it once more. Next there's a fair distance across a plateau before you dip through some snaking bends to the Langdon Beck Hotel and into the toughest part of the climb. A sharp rise bending left, but once through you can settle down for the long, wild and exposed quest to the summit.

FACTFILE

WHERE Head west out of Middleton-in-Teesdale on the B6277. Pass through Newbiggin and start the climb at the Forest-in-Teesdale sign opposite the turning to Ettersgill.

GRID REF NY 775 363 (OS92)

LENGTH 15740m

HEIGHT GAIN 312m

APPROX CLIMB TIME 42mins

A689
B6277
Ireshopeburn
BURNHOPE SEAT
F
St John's Chapel
Harwood
Langdon Beck
Ettersgill
FOREST-IN-TEESDALE
S
5km

153 CUTHBERT'S HILL

ROOKHOPE, COUNTY DURHAM

Sitting in the far north of the vast Pennines, Cuthbert's Hill is virtually the only sign of human presence on this empty moor, leading you away from the wilderness and down into Blanchland. Begin the ascent just under half a mile west of the village of Rookhope at a T-junction and head towards Blanchland. There's a short rise followed by a short dip, across a bridge and then you're up into some 20% that leads to a beautiful, sweeping right-hand bend. Following this you can sit back down for a while but it's far from easy – up ahead the road bends round to the left, eases some more and here the snow poles start. You next find yourself on a fantastic barren plateau sounded by nothing but the chattering grouse. Take some time to soak in the emptiness then follow the road up to a left-hand rise, then a right-hand dip then up again round to the left and finally to finish across a cattle grid, in this awesome middle of nowhere.

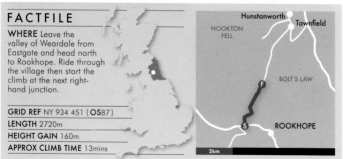

FACTFILE

WHERE Leave the valley of Weardale from Eastgate and head north to Rookhope. Ride through the village then start the climb at the next right-hand junction.

GRID REF NY 934 451 (OS87)

LENGTH 2720m

HEIGHT GAIN 160m

APPROX CLIMB TIME 13mins

154 PEAT HILL

Of the two ways out of Weardale up on to Middlehope Moor, Peat Hill out of Westgate just sneaks it as the toughest route. Leave the A689 in the centre of the village, round the first couple of houses and you're presented with a clear sight of your task. Ahead of you the ever-steepening road snakes its way through the buildings and from first sight you know it's going to be a killer, but this isn't even the toughest part. Make your way out of the village and already at maximum you'll hit the three achingly steep corners, first left then right then left again. Get through these ruthless bends, the last of which is incredibly rough, and you're almost through the worst, but there's still one more wicked stretch before the gradient relents. All that's left now is for you to follow the crooked undulating path to the summit and finish at the junction where the road heads down in either direction.

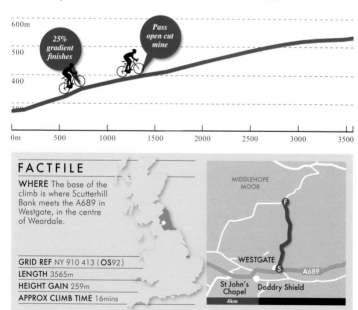

25% gradient finishes

Pass open cut mine

FACTFILE

WHERE The base of the climb is where Scutterhill Bank meets the A689 in Westgate, in the centre of Weardale.

GRID REF NY 910 413 (**OS**92)

LENGTH 3565m

HEIGHT GAIN 259m

APPROX CLIMB TIME 16mins

MIDDLEHOPE MOOR

F

WESTGATE

S   A689

St John's Chapel   Daddry Shield

4km

RATING
5/10

155 UNTHANK BANK

STANHOPE, COUNTY DURHAM

'Wow! Look at those bends.' I laughed with excitement when I first saw this road, it didn't make the cut for volume one because of its proximity to the more frequently travelled Crawleyside just opposite, but it was a hard decision to leave it out. Make your way out of Stanhope avoiding the ford if the river is high and once over a small railway line you can begin the climb. A gentle rise at first leads you to a right-hand bend then it's straight up 17% into the best set of tight snaking bends this side of the Stelvio Pass. Some climbs are great because of their length, others because of the severity of their gradient, a few more – such as Unthank Bank – are outstanding because of the character they pack into just a few hundred metres of tarmac. Bank left, up, then sweep right and, before you know it, it's over as you exit left. It's not the top, far from it, there's a lot more climbing to the summit but it's all about those twisting bends.

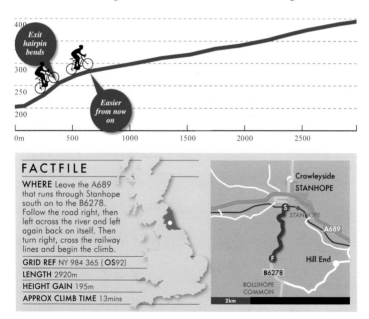

Exit hairpin bends

Easier from now on

FACTFILE

WHERE Leave the A689 that runs through Stanhope south on to the B6278. Follow the road right, then left across the river and left again back on itself. Then turn right, cross the railway lines and begin the climb.

GRID REF NY 984 365 (OS92)

LENGTH 2920m

HEIGHT GAIN 195m

APPROX CLIMB TIME 13mins

Crawleyside
STANHOPE

S
STANHOPE

A689

F
Hill End

B6278

BOLLIHOPE
COMMON

2km

156 HIGH KNOWES

I don't usually scan the map and head for anything where the contours are compact but one day I did just that and stumbled upon a beauty of a road. If you're riding the National Cycle Network Route 68 and fancy heading 'off-piste' for a while – and if you like it rugged, twisting and wild – then look no further. Turn north out of the village of Alnham, cross a cattle grid and head into a set of four hairpin bends so tangled that the road is almost tied into a knot. Following this you climb gently across a large grassy plateau, the ever deteriorating surface constantly bending left and right then delivers you to the top of a sharp drop from which point you can see the rest of the climb laid out in all its glory. This final demanding ascent takes you high into the Cheviot Hills and you finish just past the remains of an ancient fort. Unfortunately it's a dead end so you will have to double back taking extreme care in descending on the terrible surface.

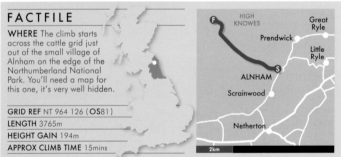

FACTFILE

WHERE The climb starts across the cattle grid just out of the small village of Alnham on the edge of the Northumberland National Park. You'll need a map for this one, it's very well hidden.

GRID REF NT 964 126 (**OS**81)	
LENGTH 3765m	
HEIGHT GAIN 194m	
APPROX CLIMB TIME 15mins	

157 CRAGPIT HILL

ROTHBURY, NORTHUMBERLAND

This hill stutters at first, climbing, levelling, dropping, but when it does settle down it hits you with a triple whammy of demanding rises that will make you very thankful to reach the moor at the top. Start on the B6341 heading east out of Rothbury and round a steep sweeping left-hand bend to a peak. Next there's some easy climbing before you drop down past the entrance to the Cragside Estate. Rounding Tumbleton Lake you hit the first of the three giant steps at a constant 16%. This is the hardest of the three and once through you've little time to recover before you almost immediately hit the second. Fortunately though, this stretch is a fraction easier than the first; the third, following a short plateau, is a touch easier still. Exiting the forest, you still have to reach the peak, which shouldn't be too much trouble – unless there's a stiff wind coming off the North Sea that is, in which case it will be hell.

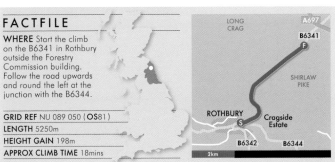

FACTFILE

WHERE Start the climb on the B6341 in Rothbury outside the Forestry Commission building. Follow the road upwards and round the left at the junction with the B6344.

GRID REF NU 089 050 (**OS**81)

LENGTH 5250m

HEIGHT GAIN 198m

APPROX CLIMB TIME 18mins

158 RYAL'S HILL

RYAL, TYNE AND WEAR

This climb is the cornerstone of the annual Beaumont Trophy bike race, one of the monuments of the British bike-racing calendar, and because of this it will always have a place in cycling folklore for the pain it has dished out. Start the climb in a hollow over a small stone bridge. There's a short ascent followed by a levelling at a crossroads then a dip down before another short, sharp rise. Following these forays you climb gently towards a farmhouse on the horizon, over the lip and you can then see one of the twin perils that await you – the dead straight road hits the first of two 1-in-6 ramps that stop you in your tracks. Grind your way up to crest the brow, crossing the faded names of riders painted on the road – and bang! – you're hit with the physiological hammer blow of having to do it all again, but thankfully this second 1-in-6 ramp is a fraction easier and you finish just past the white line painted on the road.

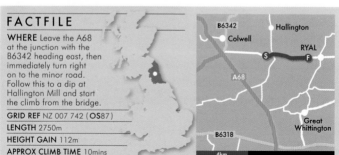

FACTFILE

WHERE Leave the A68 at the junction with the B6342 heading east, then immediately turn right on to the minor road. Follow this to a dip at Hallington Mill and start the climb from the bridge.

GRID REF NZ 007 742 (**OS87**)

LENGTH 2750m

HEIGHT GAIN 112m

APPROX CLIMB TIME 10mins

GATESHEAD, TYNE AND WEAR

If you're a cyclist living in an urban conurbation the thing you'll crave the most is a quick way out of town for an after-work ride, and more importantly somewhere decent to test your legs. For riders in the Gateshead area, Silverhills provides the perfect spot and there are two stiff climbs up the mound; the quieter, steeper and hence better of the two is Banesley Lane. To begin, leave the giant roundabout and enter the village of Lady Park, spin your legs and follow the road round to the left. At the point where the gradient begins to bite you'll notice the white line on the tarmac marking the start of the hill-climb course. There's a sharp ramp, a levelling, then following a gentle stretch hard again before you enter a smooth, wide S-bend. Exit this and you see the hard push to the top, the extremely rough road bends round to the left to a brow, a dip, a plateau then a small rise to finish at the junction.

FACTFILE

WHERE The climb starts from a giant roundabout under the A1 at the opposite side of a giant Sainsbury's south of the Chowdene area of Gateshead. Keep left past Lady Park farm as the road climbs.

GRID REF NZ 231 577 (**OS**88)

LENGTH 2285m

HEIGHT GAIN 115m

APPROX CLIMB TIME 8mins

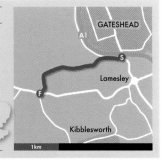

SCOTLAND

169 Bealach Ratagan

168 Glen Coe

167 Ben Lawers

170 Quiraing

165 Glen Quaich

166 Bealach Feith Nan Laogh

INVERNESS

ABERDEEN

163 Bealach Maim

162 Duke's Pass

164 Glen Finart

161 Crow Road

160 Devil's Beef Tub

GLASGOW

RATING
4/10

160 DEVIL'S BEEF TUB

MOFFAT, DUMFRIES AND GALLOWAY

What's remarkable about this climb is its unnerving ability to stick to virtually the same gradient from base to summit, all 10 kilometres of it. Head out of Moffat and begin your ascent at the rear of the town sign on the A701, the 'Scenic Trail' to Edinburgh. You will hardly notice the rise at first, pick your gear and begin to wind through countless gentle bends. The road sways left and right, never changing direction just meandering onwards and upwards. At the junction with the B719 there's the only real change in the slope, a levelling up to a pair of bends, right and then left. Through these and up ahead the beautiful hills line the horizon, rolling, effortlessly morphing into one another and as soft and smooth as giant green pillows. The equally smooth road continues to snake along, continuously climbing, steeper round the side of the hill overlooking the Beef Tub, then gradually evaporating to level and finish.

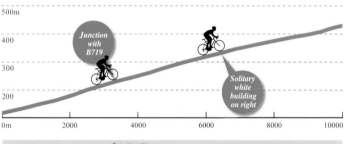

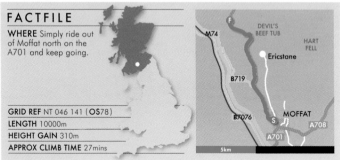

FACTFILE

WHERE Simply ride out of Moffat north on the A701 and keep going.

GRID REF NT 046 141 (OS78)

LENGTH 10000m

HEIGHT GAIN 310m

APPROX CLIMB TIME 27mins

161 CROW ROAD

LENNOXTOWN, EAST DUNBARTONSHIRE

Traversing the Campsie Fells north of Glasgow, rising out of Lennoxtown is the B822, or the Crow Road. From the base it's easy at first but as you head out of town it ramps up to 10%, if not steeper. Things ease back a touch, but only slightly as you begin the slog up the side of the mountain. The road, a single great scar on the 45-degree grassy banks slowly makes its way skyward. What few trees there were on the lower slopes are soon replaced by a single metal barrier on the left of the road, protecting you from the drop but also hemming you in. It's a relief to reach the 90-degree right turn where the road opens up a little, gentle past the car park but then comes the hardest stretch. Give it all you've got because once up this short rise it's a doddle to the top. If the wind's blowing in the right direction stick it in the big ring and pick up speed to ride the rest of the way to the border between East and West Dunbartonshire.

FACTFILE

WHERE Leave the A891 in the town of Lennoxtown and head north on the B822.

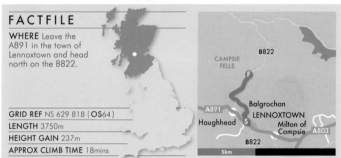

GRID REF NS 629 818 (OS64)

LENGTH 3750m

HEIGHT GAIN 237m

APPROX CLIMB TIME 18mins

162 DUKE'S PASS

A fantastic road rising through the Achray Forest into the heart of the beautiful Trossachs National Park that serves up its climbing in multiple stages. Leave Aberfoyle as the A821 bends right on to Hillside, ride right up through the houses and then follow the road left to the entrance of David Marshall Lodge. The slope eases into a majestic sweeping right-hand bend, then straight away into a left-hander but now climbing up hard again, snaking through the forest. Up to the next tight corners you now have stunning views over to your right before the road heads away from them back upwards to the plateau at the Duke's Pass sign. Here you could let your legs recover, or wind it up to the base of the last of the climbing through the rocky landscape making its way round to the right. This final long stretch isn't too tough and you roll to a finish just past the entrance to the Achray Forest Drive, then into the brilliant descent to Loch Achray.

FACTFILE

WHERE The climb starts in the centre of Aberfoyle where the B829 and the A821 meet. Although it looks like a T-junction, the A821 actually continues round the corner; follow this and head on up.

GRID REF NN 524 045 (**OS**57)

LENGTH 4040m

HEIGHT GAIN 225m

APPROX CLIMB TIME 18mins

163 BEALACH MAIM

CLACHAN OF GLENDARUEL, ARGYLL AND BUTE

A good way to sum up this climb would be to say the eastern face is Cinderella and the western face, documented here, is one, if not both, of the ugly sisters. It's rough and relentless, the surface is broken and overgrown with grass, the corners are brutal and it's a full-on arduous struggle from base to summit. Start from the small bridge at the bottom, ride up to, and past, some farm buildings, then as the rippled surface turns a distinctive red colour, the gradient begins to bite. Steep, then steeper, up to almost 20% and then into what may be Scotland's steepest corner. It's 30% at the apex and once you make it round, things don't get any easier. The road, now characterized by a foot of grass growing on the crown, is wild in every sense. Keep climbing, bend after bend, yes there are a few let-ups, but nothing significant until you approach the summit and finally as the surface improves you come to a halt. Ugly doesn't even come close.

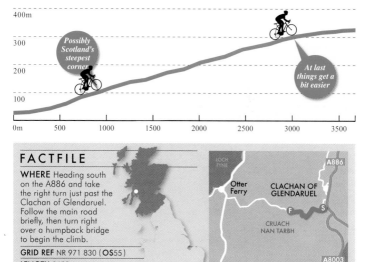

Possibly Scotland's steepest corner

At last things get a bit easier

FACTFILE

WHERE Heading south on the A886 and take the right turn just past the Clachan of Glendaruel. Follow the main road briefly, then turn right over a humpback bridge to begin the climb.

GRID REF NR 971 830 (OS55)

LENGTH 3680m

HEIGHT GAIN 299m

APPROX CLIMB TIME 18mins

LOCH FYNE

Otter Ferry

CLACHAN OF GLENDARUEL

CRUACH NAN TARBH

Kilfinan

A886

A8003

5km

164 GLEN FINART

You would expect a road through a glen, or 'valley', to be flat – the easiest way between places – but this is Scotland and this glen has a serious climb in it. Ride out of Ardentinny, through Barnacabber, and then begin to climb alongside the second of two large totem-like black and white poles on the left. Gentle at first then, past more poles and a faded 1-in-5 sign, things start to get interesting. Across a bridge and you're climbing hard, not quite 1-in-5 yet, but close, and soon you've a short levelling before the proper action begins. You sweep left into a long bend – follow the road as it arcs right then have a breather as it eases again. Ahead you can see your task etched into the landscape. Right, straight, steep then very steep left – more like 1-in-4 – round this and push yourself to a pronounced crest in the road. It's not the top, though – dip down round a protruding rock face then up again to finish at a passing place on the brow.

FACTFILE

WHERE Heading north on the A880 along the shore of Loch Long, ride through Ardentinny and Barnacabber then start to climb as the gradient increases.

GRID REF NS 151 922 (OS56)

LENGTH 2380m

HEIGHT GAIN 145m

APPROX CLIMB TIME 11mins

BARNACABBER
Ardentinny
Coulport
Benmore
LOCH
LONG
A815
A880
B833
Ardbeg
5km

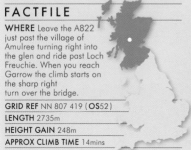

I've chosen the easier side of this climb. The north ascent is at least twice as long and a relentless grind from base to summit, but the south side, the south side is just magic. The spell is cast as you approach, riding through the glen, up ahead you see a dark line rising over the hillside. At first glance it resembles a stone wall, but it's too wide, it couldn't be the climb, surely not, that would be insane. As you get closer, it slowly starts to dawn on you that it is in fact the road, and your heart begins to thump. Starting from the small bridge at the base it's steep straight away and the surface is just beautiful, as smooth as rolled icing. The slope eases past trees on your left then it's hard up to the first cattle grid before backing off a little on the approach to the right – left switchbacks. Through these and it's steep all the way to the second cattle grid where there's a final lull in the action before one last vicious ramp that takes you to the summit.

FACTFILE

WHERE Leave the A822 just past the village of Amulree turning right into the glen and ride past Loch Freuchie. When you reach Garrow the climb starts on the sharp right turn over the bridge.

GRID REF NN 807 419 (OS52)

LENGTH 2735m

HEIGHT GAIN 248m

APPROX CLIMB TIME 14mins

166 BEALACH FEITH NAN LAOGH

SCOTSTOWN, HIGHLAND

This climb takes a while to get going but stick with it, because at the end of the rainbow lies pure climbing gold. Starting at the turn to Aryundle, it's tough for a while before easing as you pass the many scattered houses along the hillside. Up a bit, levelling, then up a bit more, after every stretch of climbing there's somewhere to recover. Across a cattle grid, the road takes you past the final buildings and into what you came to find. A myriad of steep bends lie in front of you, cutting their way through the harsh rocky landscape. Through the first batch and you're placed at the base of a leg-breaking straight that gets steeper and steeper. You've a brief easing round the corner at the top then it gets steeper still, up to 1-in-4, before turning left where you can afford yourself a chance to survey what you've conquered. Now switching back, right, left, then climbing all the way to reach its peak next to an antenna at the brow.

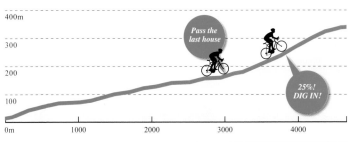

Pass the last house

25%! DIG IN!

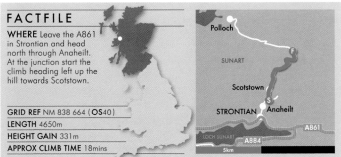

FACTFILE

WHERE Leave the A861 in Strontian and head north through Anaheilt. At the junction start the climb heading left up the hill towards Scotstown.

GRID REF NM 838 664 (**OS**40)

LENGTH 4650m

HEIGHT GAIN 331m

APPROX CLIMB TIME 18mins

Polloch

SUNART

Scotstown

STRONTIAN   Anaheilt

A861

LOCH SUNART   A884

5km

167 BEN LAWERS

BRIDGE OF BALGIE, PERTH AND KINROSS

A long, long climb on many surfaces with many gradients, nothing too steep but there's plenty of it. Start from the entrance to the Meggernie outdoor activity centre and rise up to cross the first cattle grid. The early slopes are gentle as they wind this way and that, towards a small wooded area where the tarmac changes colour and the gradient eases yet more. Leaving the trees behind you, cross a second cattle grid then the slope ramps up, and you climb, twisting and snaking, round each corner the views into the valley becoming grander and grander. You're never overwhelmed by the task though, as it's always a short distance between corners, this refreshes your mind and allows you to tackle each stretch as a separate task. And as an added bonus, the closer you get to the top, the easier the gradient. You can now pick up some real speed to finish at the brow just shy of a small blue sign next to a pile of stones.

FACTFILE

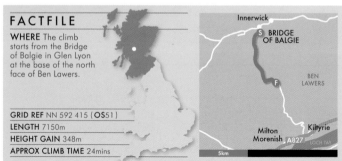

WHERE The climb starts from the Bridge of Balgie in Glen Lyon at the base of the north face of Ben Lawers.

GRID REF NN 592 415 (**OS**51)

LENGTH 7150m

HEIGHT GAIN 348m

APPROX CLIMB TIME 24mins

Innerwick

S BRIDGE OF BALGIE

BEN LAWERS

Milton Morenish

Kiltyrie

A827 LOCH TAY

5km

Often voted the most beautiful and spectacular location in the whole of Britain, you can't fail to be in awe of your surroundings as you climb the Pass of Glen Coe. Leave the banks of Loch Leven and head out on the long, flat approach. Weaving right and left following the river it's quite a while before there is a noticeable increase in gradient, but you are climbing. Following the small Loch Achtriochtan, the valley opens up but there's still no serious increase in gradient, it's only when you see the pass heading to the giant V on the horizon that you feel it bite. The higher you climb the more the road winds as it avoids huge outcrops of rock and at one point cuts straight through one. Passing the numerous viewing points, cascading waterfalls and even the odd isolated building, you finish this – the most wonderful of roads – on the heavenly giant plateau at the top.

FACTFILE

WHERE Start the climb at the junction of the B863 and the A82 and then follow the A82 east all the way to the top.

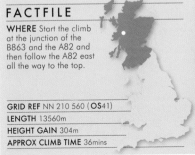

GRID REF NN 210 560 (OS41)

LENGTH 13560m

HEIGHT GAIN 304m

APPROX CLIMB TIME 36mins

169 BEALACH RATAGAN

RATAGAN, HIGHLAND

Without doubt this is as close to an Alpine pass that I have found in Britain, it's the spitting image of the Col du Télégraphe – shorter, but easily as steep, if not steeper. Begin from the cattle grid on the flat plain at the base of Loch Duich and head up the rugged surface past the turning to Ratagan village. After the turn, the surface worsens, but soon clears up as the narrow road heads inland and away from the shores of the Loch. The climb sweeps its way between the tall dark conifers, and you'll soon have to start clicking down the gears as the slope approaches 15%. Through a sharp hairpin right, things ease back for a while before you're forced into a huge, steep, left-hand bend. After this it's right, then hard going, out of the saddle all the way until the road turns left to a viewpoint. Pause to take in the majestic views of the mountains reflected in the loch then click up the gears and head right to roll to the finish at a passing place.

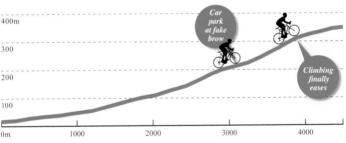

FACTFILE

WHERE To find the base leave the A87 at Shiel Bridge. Head south-west, round to the right then start the climb as you cross the cattle grid.

GRID REF NG 901 197 (OS33)

LENGTH 4460m

HEIGHT GAIN 334m

APPROX CLIMB TIME 19mins

RATING
5/10

170 QUIRAING

Atop the Isle of Skye lies a road so stunning you'll never want it to end, the grandeur of its final bends simply have no comparison in these isles. Start from the junction at the bottom, straight away steep, up and away from the scattered houses of Brogaig. Next take care to stay right at a confusing junction and continue to climb up to a cattle grid, after this the road levels and you cross a plateau beneath the jagged peaks in this mystical scenery. Bumping up and down slightly, pass a small cemetery, then into a hard, straight, 15% stretch to the fantastic corners at the top. First left, rocks jutting up either side of you, boulders strewn along the roadside, then back on yourself and into the hardest climbing. However, nothing can spoil your enjoyment of these bends set in this wonderful amphitheatre. Finally you turn sharp left, then all too soon, the gradient eases and you reach the summit where you're simply left wanting more.

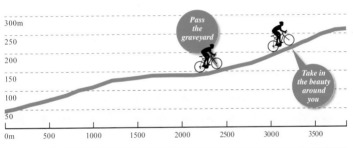

Pass the graveyard

Take in the beauty around you

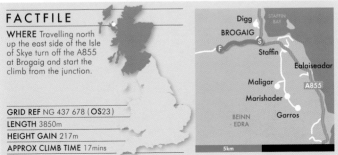

FACTFILE

WHERE Travelling north up the east side of the Isle of Skye turn off the A855 at Brogaig and start the climb from the junction.

GRID REF NG 437 678 (OS23)

LENGTH 3850m

HEIGHT GAIN 217m

APPROX CLIMB TIME 17mins

Digg   STAFFIN BAY

BROGAIG

Staffin

Ealaiseadar

Maligar

Marishader

BEINN EDRA

Garros

A855

5km

NORTH-WEST

182 Blea Tarn

181 The Struggle

184 Dowgang Hush

180 Burn Edge

185 Killhope Cross

179 Kiln Bank Cross

CARLISLE

186 Great Dun Fell

178 Bank House Moor

183 Shot Moss

177 White Shaw Moss

LIVERPOOL

176 Newton Fell

175 Whalley Nab

173 Chew Road

174 Crown Point

172 Knott Hill Lane

171 Pym Chair

171 PYM CHAIR

MACCLESFIELD, CHESHIRE

I'm setting the start of this climb at the bridge over Todd Brook outside Saltersford Hall, but there is an argument that it could be taken from the bottom of the rough Bank Lane. Either way, following an initial steep rise you arrive at the plateau on the corner outside the solitary Jenkin Chapel. Up on the horizon you'll see Pym Chair where the road cuts its way through the top of the ridge; it's going to be quite a battle to get there. Following the chapel it's hard for a while before easing then plunging back into the tough stuff past Pym Chair Farm and round a sweeping left-hand bend. The road is framed by high grassy banks and stone walls offering shelter and creating an amphitheatre-like atmosphere in which to ride. It's tough from here to the top, bending right it ramps up into the hardest stretch, up to 20%, then eases further round to the right to finish just shy of the next junction on your left.

FACTFILE

WHERE To find the base turn off the A537 signposted Saltersford. Ride down the very steep lane, up and past the reservoir then right at the junction and down to the base.

GRID REF SJ 994 776 (**OS**109)

LENGTH 1550m

HEIGHT GAIN 157m

APPROX CLIMB TIME 9mins

B5470

Nab End

LAMALOAD RESERVOIR

SHINING TOR

A537

2km

DELPH, OLDHAM

Picking a line through the holes, ridges and debris on the lower slopes of this gnarled lane is like trying to navigate an asteroid field. Starting where Knott Hill Lane leaves Stoneswood Road the climb is narrow, rugged, littered with crevasses and covered with obstacles, but to begin with at least, the gradient isn't too harsh. Twisting gently past houses on either side things soon change as you reach a hard right–left S-bend. Look for a clean line to get some traction and propel yourself through in the shadow of the high grassy bank. Once you've negotiated these stiff corners the task eases a little and after a few more scattered houses the road morphs into Hill Top Lane. You're treated to a slight plateau then it's into a more substantial gradient that leads you up on to the exposed moor; it's a true battle to reach the summit of this great road but once you make it the view in all directions is more than worth the effort.

FACTFILE

WHERE From the A6052 passing through the centre of Delph turn off up Stoneswood Road past the Millgate Arts Centre. Climb hard round to the right then take the first right turn.

GRID REF SD 971 078 (OS109)

LENGTH 1800m

HEIGHT GAIN 133m

APPROX CLIMB TIME 8mins

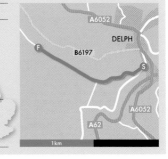

RATING
8/10

173 CHEW ROAD

GREENFIELD, OLDHAM

This is no ordinary road and there are plenty of reasons why I shouldn't have included it in the book, but these pale into insignificance compared with the joy of climbing it. For starters, only half of the road is paved, and on top of this there's a gate to traverse about midway up. Let's ignore these minor issues though. To reach the base, pass the reservoir car park and the sailing club, cross a small bridge and you're ready to start. The adventure kicks off with a smooth 20% ramp to get the legs and lungs burning, and then you alternate a while between a smooth new surface and a damaged old one. Following a short levelling, the next obstacle presents itself in the form of jarring stone drainage channels. From now on, every 20 metres or so, your progress is checked as you rumble across these uncomfortable lumps. With the valley opening up, the road lies dead centre snaking its way through the stunning barren scenery, and it's here that the surface turns to loose gravel. I was annoyed at first, but then I was reminded of the photos of those pioneering Tour de France riders as they first crossed the unsealed Pyrenean passes in the early 1900s. In my mind I was now scaling the Col du Tourmalet, fighting the gradient, the elements and the surface. Next is the gate: don't be put off, scale it, remount and soon the surface is sealed once more, then track, then finally sealed for the approach to the summit. It's empty, quiet, and the climbing is tough as you pass the huge angled boulders that line the route. Eventually you will see in front of you the dead straight horizon punctuated by a lone tower. There's one final wickedly steep rise following a 90-degree bend before you finish at the reservoir in the sky on the top of Saddleworth Moor. Simply *epic*.

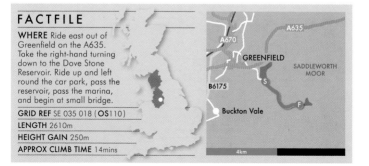

FACTFILE

WHERE Ride east out of Greenfield on the A635. Take the right-hand turning down to the Dove Stone Reservoir. Ride up and left round the car park, pass the reservoir, pass the marina, and begin at small bridge.

GRID REF SE 035 018 (OS110)

LENGTH 2610m

HEIGHT GAIN 250m

APPROX CLIMB TIME 14mins

174 CROWN POINT

BURNLEY, OLDHAM

There are two ways to start this climb
and I've chosen the one that's raced
in hill climbs, Woodplumpton Road
which heads south from the A646. This
forms the first half of the route to the
summit and is also the toughest section
to climb. A short distance in and you
pass a familiar faded white line in the
left-hand gutter that marks the starting
point for the raced distance. The surface
on this quiet lane is generally good but
becomes rough and patchy in places;
after passing a gate on your right the
gradient steepens. The road passes
through tall grassy banks and high stone
walls until the gradient begins to lessen
and you approach the right-hand bend
at the top, and the second white line,
marking the finish. From here join the
larger Crown Point Road, turning left
and across a cattle grid, down a slight
dip, winding right before climbing left
up the long 10% exposed road to the
summit on the moor.

FACTFILE

WHERE The base of the
climb is on Woodplumpton
Road where it joins the
A646 on the south side
of Burnley.

GRID REF SD 849 282 (OS103)

LENGTH 2980m

HEIGHT GAIN 147m

APPROX CLIMB TIME 14mins

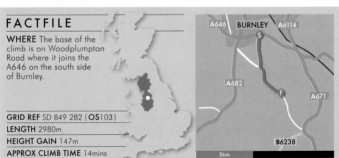

WHALLEY, LANCASHIRE

This isn't a road to slot casually into your evening ride. It's either to be avoided or left for those special days when you're really feeling good. It starts so viciously steep, it's like a rocket taking off; it is the very definition of a Killer Climb. From the junction you've seconds to click into your smallest sprocket and wham! You hit the giant, arcing, 25% right-hand bend. Round the corner it eases very little and within a couple of hundred metres you're already high above Whalley. The road kinks left, there's a slight shallowing, then it straightens, and it's wickedly steep once more. A little further along and it backs off just enough for you to cast your eyes over the viaduct below, but up to, and past, some houses it's super-tough again. From here you'll inch upwards, easing, then climbing, twisting through the trees all the way until you pass a dead-end junction on your left and you reach the summit as Moor Lane turns into Shawcliffe Lane.

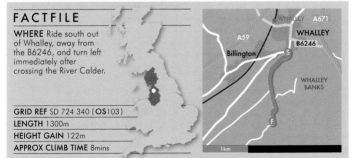

FACTFILE

WHERE Ride south out of Whalley, away from the B6246, and turn left immediately after crossing the River Calder.

GRID REF SD 724 340 (OS103)

LENGTH 1300m

HEIGHT GAIN 122m

APPROX CLIMB TIME 8mins

RATING
7/10

176 NEWTON FELL

Like Bowland Knotts, this is another climb that had me wondering what the fuss was all about on the early slopes, only to have me eating my words once I'd reached the top. Start as you cross the River Hodder – the road kinks right into a dead straight, wide, even, and steep gradient. I prefer lots of corners and really hate this type of slope, psychologically they are always much tougher to ride. Over the brow and mercifully the road dips down to bisect a farm, climbs, then almost levels up to some houses where it's tough again. Riding away from the last of the trees into open land you make your way to a cattle grid and a rather underwhelming summit. Yet it's not the top: round the blind bend and you see you're nowhere close. Dip down to a short, sharp rise lined with stone walls, the steepest part of the whole climb, then begin the long, exposed journey to the summit at a parking place before a cattle grid.

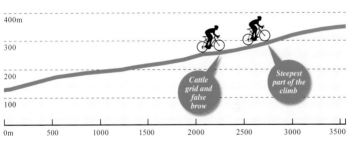

Cattle grid and false brow

Steepest part of the climb

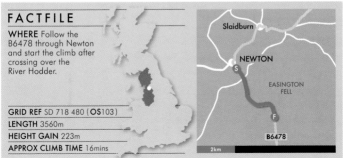

FACTFILE

WHERE Follow the B6478 through Newton and start the climb after crossing over the River Hodder.

Slaidburn

NEWTON

EASINGTON FELL

B6478

2km

GRID REF SD 718 480 (OS103)

LENGTH 3560m

HEIGHT GAIN 223m

APPROX CLIMB TIME 16mins

177 WHITE SHAW MOSS

DEEPDALE, CUMBRIA

It's so beautiful at the top of this climb, I'd have sat there, weather permitting, all day, mesmerized by the emptiness, the barren hillsides only tainted by the thin stone walls that partition them. Beginning just outside the village of Deepdale, the road rises gently at first then gets stiffer through some bends, then, unfortunately, there's a gate. Even more unfortunately, however, is the fact that as soon as you're through the gate you have to remount on a 20% slope and attack the steepest part of the climb. A fantastic pair of sharp left, then right, bends that lead you to another hard left, followed by some easier climbing up to the second and final gate. Through this, in the now desolate landscape, you head to a brow as the road bends right round the hillside, but it's not the top – not yet. There's a brief plateau, then another, near identical, right-hand bend that does deliver you to the summit at a small parking place as the road bends right.

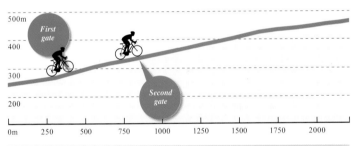

FACTFILE

WHERE Ride through Dent in Dentdale, then turn south, up and over into Deepdale. Start the climb out of the village across a small bridge in front of a waterfall.

GRID REF SD 722 818 (OS98)

LENGTH 2215m

HEIGHT GAIN 221m

APPROX CLIMB TIME 14mins

KIRKBY-IN-FURNESS, CUMBRIA

There are two roads to the top of Bank House Moor; the one out of Soutergate is so rough in places it's little more than a track so I chose the climb out of Beck Side. Start outside the church gates, ride through the village and make sure you follow the road as it bends 90 degrees right (signposted Ulverston). Once through this junction you've two bends, tight left then right, but not especially steep, then solid climbing up to the first cattle grid. Now I say cattle grid, and I've ridden across enough of them, but this one – this one's more like some hideous medieval trap. I chickened out and climbed the gate. Back on the bike you're into a wicked stretch of gradient gradually bending round to the left – a really solid, steep slog that ends as the road kinks right. Next there's a little drop, line yourself up to cross the next, this time standard, cattle grid then another steep rise up to and across a third and final grid to finish at the brow.

FACTFILE

WHERE Head east away from the A595 in Kirkby-in-Furness and start the climb outside the church in Beck Side.

GRID REF SD 247 810 (**OS**96)	
LENGTH 2150m	
HEIGHT GAIN 223m	
APPROX CLIMB TIME 12mins	

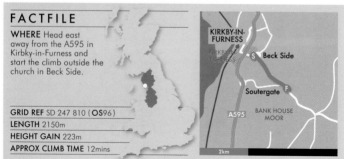

KIRKBY-IN-FURNESS

Beck Side

Soutergate

A595   BANK HOUSE MOOR

2km

The climb up Stickle Pike to Kiln Bank Cross starts at the gate to the Ulpha water treatment works; immediately narrow, framed by gigantic stone walls it soon gets steep leading to a slight plateau. Next a dip and under the only bit of tree cover, past farm buildings and steep out of the trees up to a cattle grid. Build momentum to cross it and ride into a wickedly sharp left-hand bend, then another hard right into a long steep stretch framed by more giant walls. The size of the stones at the base is quite astonishing, they're not of human scale; it's as if giants placed them there long ago. Up ahead you see a white gate, use this as a point of focus, about halfway the slope recedes a little, passing through a small group of trees then it's steep again to the gate. Pass over a cattle grid and it's now a bit easier to the top, the road cutting its way across the spectacularly jagged landscape to peak at a parking place.

FACTFILE

WHERE Begin the climb in the valley formed by the River Duddon. Head south from Hall Dunnerdale and begin opposite the entrance to the Ulpha water works.

GRID REF SD 214 932 (OS96)

LENGTH 1810m

HEIGHT GAIN 177m

APPROX CLIMB TIME 11mins

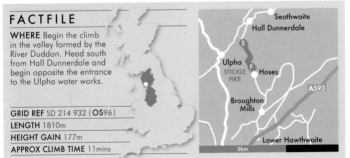

180 BURN EDGE

ENNERDALE BRIDGE, CUMBRIA

Even when you reach the top of Burn Edge you still won't believe it, it cries wolf so many times you just resign yourself to the fact that you will be climbing for a very long time. Kicking off a little way out of Ennerdale Bridge, you start with the steep, straight ramp of Scarny Brow, which eases as it approaches some woods on the left. Levelling past the trees you arrive at the climb's beauty spot, a wonderful set of sweeping bends, as kind on the eyes as they are hard on the legs. Push through, across a cattle grid, and on to the open moor, up to a brow, level, then rise gently before dropping as the road bends left. Next you see the road disappear into the distance and it's really tough to the brow, but once reached things ease up before you head left. As the road rounds the next corner, once again it disappears over yet another horizon, still climbing, round the next right and you're almost there, just a few hundred metres to top-out just shy of a wood.

FACTFILE

WHERE Leave the village of Ennerdale Bridge heading towards Cleator Moor and the A5086. At the first junction turn south to start the climb.

GRID REF NY 064 123 (OS89)

LENGTH 3750m

HEIGHT GAIN 167m

APPROX CLIMB TIME 14mins

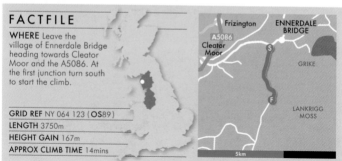

181 THE STRUGGLE

AMBLESIDE, CUMBRIA

There are three ways to the inn at the top of the Kirkstone Pass, either way up the A592 and the third, out of Ambleside along Kirkstone Road, the wonderfully named 'Struggle'. The road is immediately very steep but silky smooth as it winds out of the town past a sign warning of the dangerous winter conditions. The surface of the now very narrow 17% incline soon deteriorates though and is littered with large potholes and repairs. Weaving between the high drystone walls, the road next flattens, followed by a short downhill, climbs again briefly and into a second descent, then, there in front of you is 'The Struggle'. A wicked, twisting collection of eight sharp turns, the tarmac concertinas up the ridge to the inn. Climbing ever steeper, the vicious corners deliver you to the last 50 metres of 20%, then finally to the junction where in all directions the only way is down.

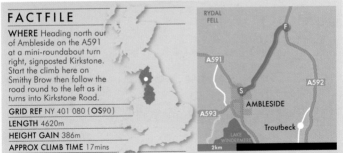

FACTFILE

WHERE Heading north out of Ambleside on the A591 at a mini-roundabout turn right, signposted Kirkstone. Start the climb here on Smithy Brow then follow the road round to the left as it turns into Kirkstone Road.

GRID REF NY 401 080 (OS90)

LENGTH 4620m

HEIGHT GAIN 386m

APPROX CLIMB TIME 17mins

RATING
8/10

182 BLEA TARN

If hills were women then the climb up to Blea Tarn would be a supermodel – it's so beautiful, its curves so luscious, so photogenic. Somebody throw some cold water over me! Start in the breathtaking valley outside a campsite just over a small stone bridge and climb gradually to a narrowing of the road, cross the obligatory cattle grid and, equally rife in this part of England, pass the 25% sign. The well-sealed but extremely lumpy road is super-tough right away as it makes its way to the first set of arduous but fantastic left- then right-hand bends. Through these and it's immediately left and right again. Although very steep, all the twisting and turning reduces the impact of the gradient, psychologically at least. Following this set of bends, the road veers left. Head for the peak on the horizon and at its base bend right to finish with a flourish up to the top for a view over to the pristine little tarn.

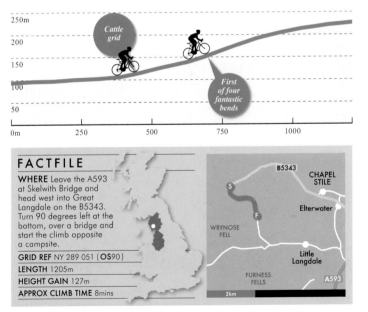

FACTFILE

WHERE Leave the A593 at Skelwith Bridge and head west into Great Langdale on the B5343. Turn 90 degrees left at the bottom, over a bridge and start the climb opposite a campsite.

GRID REF NY 289 051 (OS90)

LENGTH 1205m

HEIGHT GAIN 127m

APPROX CLIMB TIME 8mins

183 SHOT MOSS

BROUGH, CUMBRIA

The B6726 up to Shot Moss, along with Hartside Pass 25 miles to the north, bookend the largest area of unsettled land in England. This giant clump of Pennine Fells – Mickle, Dufton, Melmerby and the infamous Great Dun – together form a vast expanse of wilderness, and you're heading right into it. To begin the climb head north from Brough and start as the road forks left, gentle at first, you pass a small white house and the gradient increases a little. Winding left and right with a few brief levellings it's not until you reach the next group of buildings that things turn ugly. This, the toughest part of the climb, is a long 11% slog fortunately followed by a considerable flat section that allows you to refresh the legs before reaching a small stone bridge and the finale. Hard work again – the road, now lined with snow poles emphasizing its hostile location, reaches its peak then rolls over a cattle grid into Teesdale.

FACTFILE

WHERE Leave Brough, just off the A66 and ride up and out of town, heading east on the B6276. Start the climb from the junction where you turn left as the road you left Brough on, bends right.

GRID REF NY 827 197 (OS92)

LENGTH 6090m

HEIGHT GAIN 264m

APPROX CLIMB TIME 21mins

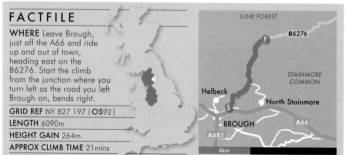

NENTHEAD, CUMBRIA

Cutting the corner up and over Middle Fell between the A689 and the B6277 is the climb of Dowgang Hush. The base lies in the small village of Nenthead and as soon as you begin, you are thrust on to its 20% slopes. The severity of this super-steep start will plunge your body into oxygen deficit and fill your legs with lactate, and there's little chance for them to recover. Steeper and steeper it rises to a pronounced lip in the road that marks the end of the tough stuff. Following this, the climbing is much easier and almost flat in places, although it's hard to appreciate it owing to the effort you've expended to get there. You're now in a position of balancing recovery from the early efforts with continuing your progress to the top. Riding higher between the stone walls the gradient begins to creep up again but not for long before levelling, and you roll to finish level with a 20% warning sign on the opposite side of the road.

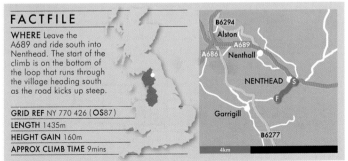

FACTFILE

WHERE Leave the A689 and ride south into Nenthead. The start of the climb is on the bottom of the loop that runs through the village heading south as the road kicks up steep.

GRID REF NY 770 426 (OS87)

LENGTH 1435m

HEIGHT GAIN 160m

APPROX CLIMB TIME 9mins

B6294
Alston
A689
A686 Nenthall
NENTHEAD S
Garrigill F
B6277
4km

185 KILLHOPE CROSS

Killhope Cross marks the high point of the A689 which bisects the North Pennines between Alston and Weardale. It's a tough climb in either direction but I've chosen to ride it west to east starting the climb in the hollow of the road outside the Nenthall Hotel. The road bends right, there's a little lump to prime the legs then it's gentle until you reach a narrow stone bridge. The road kinks right into a tough stretch of what is advertised as 13%, but seems steeper, then eases before dropping down into Nenthead. It's here that the real hard work starts – climbing 15% out of the village, the wide road bends first left, climbs hard, then right before straightening out for a minuscule amount of respite at the turning for Allenheads. Now to get to the top: first you have a 17% slog, it eases, then there's an even harder 18%, through this it eases only enough for you to look up and see the final 15% stretch to the exposed summit at the stone cross.

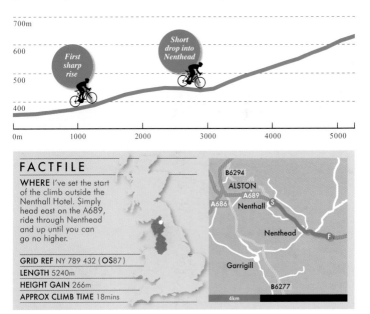

FACTFILE

WHERE I've set the start of the climb outside the Nenthall Hotel. Simply head east on the A689, ride through Nenthead and up until you can go no higher.

GRID REF	NY 789 432 (**OS**87)
LENGTH	5240m
HEIGHT GAIN	266m
APPROX CLIMB TIME	18mins

186 GREAT DUN FELL

This is the greatest climb in England, this is our Mont Ventoux, it has no peers, there is no comparison: Great Dun Fell is simply unique. I'd waited a long time to ride this road, initially put off by its 'private' status, I was to discover that there is absolutely no objection to cyclists riding it, although few would be mad enough. Approaching from either direction you see the radar station's 'golf ball' glowing like a beacon on the top of the ridge. Turn away from the village of Knock and begin opposite a farm gate. The climb is tough right away, then gets tougher still as you bend right into what is a small taste of things to come. Through this, the first of many brutal stretches, and things back off for a while before ramping up to the first of two gates. Through the gate, straight over a cattle grid and into more hard work, the road bending left past a stone shelter, a sure-fire signal – although you are nowhere near the top yet – that you're heading into truly hostile country. Up and up, then mercifully dipping, or is it just a levelling? Whatever it is, it just makes the stretch of climbing ahead look terrifying. Approaching 20%, you crawl up through the harsh, boulder-littered scenery, a massive slog to the briefest of levels where the classification of the road changes – public cars are allowed no further. Now very narrow and lined with snow poles, the climb is so well surfaced it resembles a 2-metre-wide grey carpet. And it's so steep, this time close to 25% at the point where the tall valley walls disappear and the radar slowly rises over the horizon to sit above you, tracking the remainder of your progress. Through a second gate it's easy for a while then bending right once again it's leg-breakingly tough to the finish at the station, where, looking around you, you might as well be on top of the world.

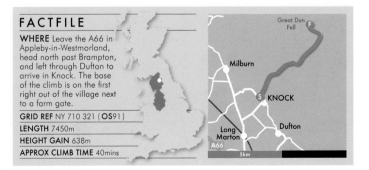

FACTFILE

WHERE Leave the A66 in Appleby-in-Westmorland, head north past Brampton, and left through Dufton to arrive in Knock. The base of the climb is on the first right out of the village next to a farm gate.

GRID REF NY 710 321 (OS91)

LENGTH 7450m

HEIGHT GAIN 638m

APPROX CLIMB TIME 40mins

WALES

189 Llanberis Pass

191 Hirnant Pass

188 Melin-y-Wig

190 Prenteg

187 Long Mountain

ABERYSTWYTH

CARDIFF

192 Dyfi Forest

193 Heol Senni

194 Gospel Pass

195 Gamallt

196 Caerphilly Mountain

197 Rhiwr Road

187 LONG MOUNTAIN

On the map, this 'little' climb doesn't look very remarkable, I rode it at the end of a long day and expected to whiz up and over no problem. How wrong I was. I simply wasn't mentally prepared for the barrage of gradient I was faced with, it just keeps coming at you again and again. Start from the junction with the A458 next to the Welsh Harp Hollow sign and ease your way past a scattering of buildings. Ride gently up to the 90-degree left-hand corner then continue up to the first test, a set of steep bends, through them, then it's gradual climbing once more. Pass a right-hand fork in the road, head straight on and dip down, it's after this that the torture begins. Up hard to a brow, easing, up to another brow, easing, time after time, a seemingly never-ending cycle of false summits, each one looking to break your resolve. Winding left and right, each sapping stretch leading you to the next, and finally, thankfully, finishing at the T-junction.

FACTFILE

WHERE Just north of Welshpool, head east from Buttington Cross on the A458. Then take the second right turn past the farm on the corner and head up Welsh Harp Hollow.

GRID REF SJ 278 077 (OS126)

LENGTH 2900m

HEIGHT GAIN 277m

APPROX CLIMB TIME 15mins

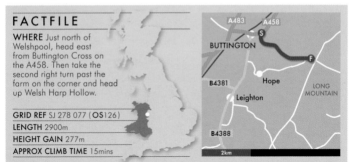

188 MELIN-Y-WIG

Tucked away in a maze of roads south of the B5105 in Denbighshire lies a little gem of a climb, hard to ride and even harder to find. Melin-y-Wig is just waiting to test the legs of weary cyclists who've strayed from the path. Leaving the village across a small bridge you head north-east climbing past the houses and into the trees. The twisting, gnarled and rugged road climbs steep, hard round to the right, then left, your wheels slipping and skidding as they struggle for traction. Easing slightly as you exit the trees but only slightly, the broken road winds its way up to a small group of farm buildings where you can have the briefest of rests before the final fireworks start. The road rears up arcing round to the left into a really tough 25% corner, your already hurting legs will not like this but you're almost at the top – bend right then roll to finish at the brow.

FACTFILE

WHERE You can find the village of Melin-y-Wig at the centre of the triangle made by the A5, A494 and the B5105. Leave the A5 at Maerdy, ride through Bettws Gwerfil Goch and into Melin, then bear right and up.

GRID REF SJ 045 498 (**OS**116)

LENGTH 1330m

HEIGHT GAIN 100m

APPROX CLIMB TIME 7mins

189 LLANBERIS PASS

LLANBERIS, GWYNEDD

So stunning is this road you half expect Gandalf the White, staff aloft, to come charging down the valley on a horse. This is truly awe-inspiring scenery. Begin the climb just outside the small village of Nant Peris with a short lip then level a bit before settling into the solid climbing. It's a while before the gradient really bites and is for the most part a sit-down climb. There are a few points where you have to leave the comfort of your saddle but these are mostly in the first third of the climb on the approach to the small bridge where the road crosses from one side of the stream to the other. Following the bridge beneath the towering banks of fallen rock, the climbing is steady again until you close in on the summit. The last couple of hundred metres are tough up to the brow outside the Pen-y-Pass Youth Hostel and the car park for walkers heading out to conquer Snowdon.

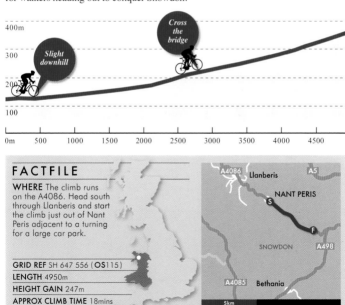

FACTFILE

WHERE The climb runs on the A4086. Head south through Llanberis and start the climb just out of Nant Peris adjacent to a turning for a large car park.

GRID REF SH 647 556 (OS115)

LENGTH 4950m

HEIGHT GAIN 247m

APPROX CLIMB TIME 18mins

190 PRENTEG

PRENTEG, GWYNEDD

You've heard the saying 'a short, sharp shock'? Well this climb is 'the long, sharp shock'; the famous Welsh leg breaker just doesn't give in. Start outside the playground at the base next to the telephone box and you're faced with a 1-in-6 sign, there's another just like it at the top, and it's pretty much 1-in-6 all the way between. Set off, pass a small car park on the right and you're climbing, bending left, left again, right then left through the houses. Next the tough, snaking road continues, lined either side with overgrown stone walls in the dark under the cover of trees. Push your way up into the daylight where it's mercifully a fraction easier as it twists and turns across an open grassy plateau. Next comes the only rest, but it's just 10 metres of flat, before the steepest corner of the lot, a wall-like left-hander, which leads you eventually up to a cattle grid where you finish alongside a four-foot-high stone wall.

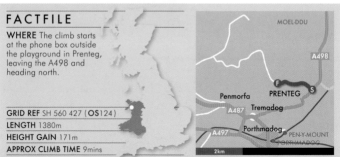

FACTFILE

WHERE The climb starts at the phone box outside the playground in Prenteg, leaving the A498 and heading north.

GRID REF SH 560 427 (OS124)

LENGTH 1380m

HEIGHT GAIN 171m

APPROX CLIMB TIME 9mins

BALA, GWYNEDD

To climb the Hirnant Pass from north to south is pure uncomplicated joy. OK, there's more climbing on the other side up from Lake Vyrnwy but this is the side to ride. This face has the drama, the vast open valley, the sheer drop, the scree-lined roadside, it has all the classic hallmarks of a mountain pass. Starting from the cattle grid in the perfectly formed valley you can see the whole climb lined out in front of you – the road, a jagged scar on the pristine landscape. You're eased into the climbing, however, with every pedal rev it gets that little bit tougher but thankfully never *too* tough. As you reach the first set of barriers you're allowed a slight rest but after this, up to, and for the duration of the second set of battered barriers the climbing is stiff. Past the last barrier and through a collection of winding bends things gradually ease up to the finish at the small car park on the brow.

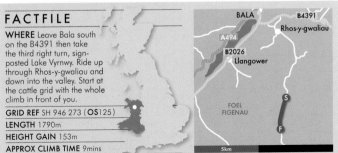

FACTFILE

WHERE Leave Bala south on the B4391 then take the third right turn, signposted Lake Vyrnwy. Ride up through Rhos-y-gwaliau and down into the valley. Start at the cattle grid with the whole climb in front of you.

GRID REF SH 946 273 (OS125)

LENGTH 1790m

HEIGHT GAIN 153m

APPROX CLIMB TIME 9mins

BALA · B4391 · Rhos-y-gwaliau · A494 · B2026 Llangower · FOEL FIGENAU · S · F · 5km

192 DYFI FOREST

ABERLLEFENNI, GWYNEDD

In the centre of a triangle of roads south of Dolgellau lies the lost world of the Dyfi Forest. Splitting the area in two, between Corris in the west and Aberangell in the east, is one hell of an isolated, lonely, forgotten road. Never had I felt so alone on the bike, if something had gone wrong out there it would have been weeks, months even, until anyone found me, I started to get flashbacks from the movie *Deliverance*, should I turn back? No. I can't, I have a hill to climb. The ascent begins across a small stone bridge as you leave Aberllefenni just before a left-hand junction and rises gently into the forest. The slope is benign to begin with – pass a few houses down a brief dip, cross a stream, then you approach a 17% gradient sign. Across a cattle grid, the road narrows and the surface deteriorates, now lined on and off with old barriers and with enough grass on the crown to make a nice lawn, it climbs up to a second cattle grid. Following this it plateaus, then after a junction on the left dips down briefly again before resuming its upward progress. As you exit the murky light under the cover of trees you round a sharp right-hand bend into the first of two stretches of 20% gradient. Relatively short but hard, then the climb ebbs and flows as the natural woods are replaced by the 'man-made' pine forest. Twisting left and right, climbing, levelling, climbing again, you reach the second stretch of 20%. This time much tougher, bending right then left – you can scream if you like, but in this forest no one will hear you. Rounding another hard left-hander, the end is approaching, you still have to climb a fair distance but from now on it's not too tough, just oh so quiet, as you roll to the finish at the final brow.

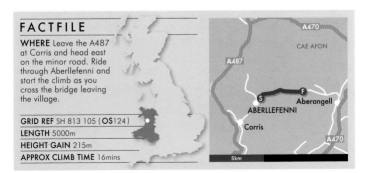

FACTFILE

WHERE Leave the A487 at Corris and head east on the minor road. Ride through Aberllefenni and start the climb as you cross the bridge leaving the village.

GRID REF SH 813 105 (OS124)

LENGTH 5000m

HEIGHT GAIN 215m

APPROX CLIMB TIME 16mins

RATING 7/10

193 HEOL SENNI

HEOL SENNI, POWYS

This is a beautifully rugged road hidden in the wild heart of the Brecon Beacons. It's a quiet route lying inbetween two busier roads and seems somewhat forgotten with its crumbling surface and neglected rusting barriers at the top. To start, leave the small village of Heol Senni, follow the river south and begin the climb adjacent to a right-hand junction. Stay left and head on up. The narrow, gnarled strip of now very rough tarmac climbs and winds through twisted trees either side easing a pinch as you cross the first of two cattle grids. You feel like you're in a truly isolated wilderness as the road gradually climbs steeper approaching the two wicked hairpins; first sharp left, then sharp right with a really tough stretch between them. Round the second hairpin and it eases to finish at the brow – the beauty of your surroundings will mask any pain. If only all roads were as quiet and wonderful as this.

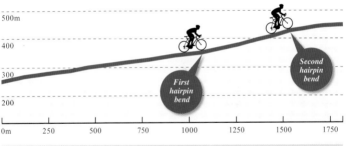

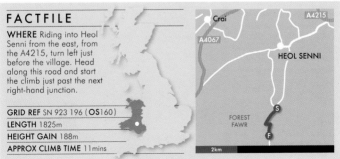

FACTFILE

WHERE Riding into Heol Senni from the east, from the A4215, turn left just before the village. Head along this road and start the climb just past the next right-hand junction.

GRID REF SN 923 196 (OS160)

LENGTH 1825m

HEIGHT GAIN 188m

APPROX CLIMB TIME 11mins

194 GOSPEL PASS

The toughest climbing on the Gospel Pass comes at the bottom, hidden amongst the trees of Tack Wood. I liken this climb to getting the housework done before you're allowed out to ride – drag your bike and body through the tough lower slopes, put in the hard graft, and you'll be rewarded with the amazing vistas and the easier ride to the summit. Begin 4 kilometres south of Hay-on-Wye at a small triangular junction and follow the road round to the right as it begins its ascent into the woods ahead. It's a narrow and very well-surfaced road, snaking left, right, and significantly steep in places. Over the final punishing rise of the bottom section, riding away from the last of the trees, the scenery opens up and you can see the path winding into the distance. There is still a long way to go, and at the finish, just to remind you it's a proper hill, the last few bends ramp up to give you one final test.

FACTFILE

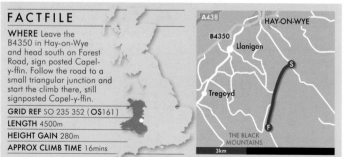

WHERE Leave the B4350 in Hay-on-Wye and head south on Forest Road, sign posted Capel-y-ffin. Follow the road to a small triangular junction and start the climb there, still signposted Capel-y-ffin.

GRID REF SO 235 352 (OS161)

LENGTH 4500m

HEIGHT GAIN 280m

APPROX CLIMB TIME 16mins

A438
HAY-ON-WYE
B4350
Llanigon
Tregoyd
S
F
THE BLACK MOUNTAINS
3km

195 GAMALLT

ABERGWESYN, POWYS

Although not quite the middle of nowhere, this can't be far from it. Following the road on from the Devil's Staircase, heading towards Tregaron, you'll encounter another vicious, gnarled and weather-beaten climb, and one that was famous for forcing riders off their bikes during the Milk Race in the 1980s. Although with modern bikes and better gearing you won't have the same problem, I hope. Begin the climb as you cross the River Towy. The very narrow road turns right, the rough and broken surface then bends a wickedly sharp left. You next hit a tortuous 25% section, the tarmac deteriorating at the edges as nature seeks to remove all trace of man. Drag yourself up this stretch over a false brow then round to the left, left again and into more 20% climbing. The short sharp shocks of the lower slopes are now over and you'll soon be bending right and climbing gently over the top and back towards signs of civilization.

FACTFILE

WHERE You'll find this nasty little beast on the tiny road between Abergwesyn and Tregaron. However, heading west from Abergwesyn you'll unfortunately have to ride the Devil's Staircase first. Sorry.

GRID REF SN 798 573 (**OS**147)

LENGTH 870m

HEIGHT GAIN 67m

APPROX CLIMB TIME 5mins

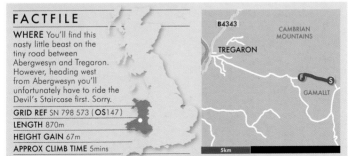

CAERPHILLY

The Mountain Road out of Caerphilly might not be able to hold a flame to the many great mountain passes across Wales but in the densely populated area around Cardiff and Newport it offers a significant test for those cyclists who regularly ride it. There are other ways to reach this peak. The A469 out of Cardiff has a few wickedly steep spots but it's a horribly busy road. There is also the much quieter Wenallt Road also heading north. However, the best way to ride is south out of Caerphilly up the B4623. It's an uncomplicated road, you begin outside the train station and head straight up through the outskirts of the small town. The gradient is all but uniform the whole way up which makes it a proper grind, reaching its steepest shortly before a large parking area on your left. Keep pushing on as the road bends gently right then finally steep left to finish at the Caerphilly Mountain snack bar.

FACTFILE

WHERE Start the climb from the centre of Caerphilly outside the railway station and head south and up Mountain Road, the B4623.

GRID REF ST 155 852 (OS171)

LENGTH 1450m

HEIGHT GAIN 135m

APPROX CLIMB TIME 7mins

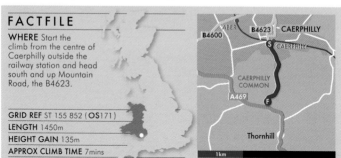

197 RHIWR ROAD

CLYDACH, GWENT

You'll be hard pushed to find a tougher climb anywhere in south Wales: this is an utter beast. There are more arrows on this road than in an archer's quiver. Head off in the shadow of a very impressive tree house in front of the 1-in-5 sign on a small bridge. It's steep but not too steep to begin with – certainly not 1-in-5 – as you make your way to a small plateau in front of an old red phone box. Enjoy this moment's rest then kiss your saddle goodbye. Follow the narrow road as it continues hard through the village up to the Cambrian Inn. It's here where things get nasty as you bank left into an epically steep, lung-busting, stretch of climbing, closer to 1-in-4, than the 1-in-5 advertised, only easing when you exit the trees. From here to the summit there's very little variation in gradient, it's all hard. Grind your way up the straights and through the tight corners slumping to a finish outside the Jolly Colliers Free House.

FACTFILE

WHERE Heading west on the A465 from Govilon, turn right signposted Clydach South and Llanelly Hill. Ride along the flat past a small park and begin the climb as the road bends left past a 1-in-5 sign.

GRID REF SO 224 121 (**OS**161)

LENGTH 1660m

HEIGHT GAIN 208m

APPROX CLIMB TIME 10mins

ISLE OF MAN

198 Bungalow

200 Snaefell Mountain

RAMSEY

DOUGLAS

199 Injebreck Hill

SULBY GLEN, ISLE OF MAN

If you want to avoid speeding motorcycles on the TT course, in fact any traffic at all up to the top of Snaefell, then this is the route for you. Start the ride from a near-idyllic setting, on the bridge over a crystal-clear stream opposite a small stone chapel and ride headlong into the toughest part of the climb. You're faced with a cluster of 14% hairpin bends, not evil, but a serious bit of climbing, right, then hairpin left. You must ride wide as it's too steep at the apex. Next bend right, then you're led left to continue on the gruelling 14% gradient for some time. The road twists and turns and there is no letup until you hit a cattle grid, cross this and it's a whole new ball game. The surface suddenly improves and the slope eases, the seemingly omnipresent Snaefell looms high above you as you are allowed to churn out a decent rhythm to finish at the Bungalow station at the T-junction.

FACTFILE

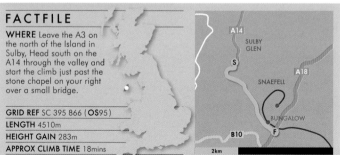

WHERE Leave the A3 on the north of the Island in Sulby, Head south on the A14 through the valley and start the climb just past the stone chapel on your right over a small bridge.

GRID REF SC 395 866 (**OS**95)	
LENGTH 4510m	
HEIGHT GAIN 283m	
APPROX CLIMB TIME 18mins	

BALDWIN, ISLE OF MAN

This hill has a bit of everything, and it's as quiet a road as you'll find anywhere in Britain. Start the climb over the bridge in the centre of Baldwin and head up quite steeply at first before rolling up and down until you reach the reservoir, where it levels. Past the northern tip of the water things start to get tougher and in no time you're faced with the first serious challenge, a very steep hairpin that delivers you into a wicked stretch of 20%. The next obstacle is a cattle grid set in the 20% gradient and you've got to give it everything to smoothly negotiate the bars. Bending left it eases a bit as you head for open land, the roadside lined with gnarled and twisted trees jutting from the high grassy banks. After an age on the abrasive steep slopes you reach a short plateau, cross a second cattle grid then enter a fantastic set of zig zag bends, left, hard right then left to finish at the brow in sight of Snaefell.

FACTFILE

WHERE Riding out of Douglas on the A23 pass through Strang, then turn right on to the B22 signposted Baldwin. Once in the village, now called West Baldwin, start opposite the right-hand turn to East Baldwin.

GRID REF SC 351 860 (**OS**95)

LENGTH 5400m

HEIGHT GAIN 305m

APPROX CLIMB TIME 21mins

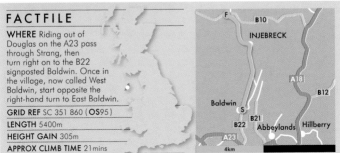

RATING
7/10

RAMSEY, ISLE OF MAN

This famous stretch of the Isle of Man TT route takes you from shore to sky up a road that packs in all gradients and surfaces. Start your ascent in the centre of Ramsey, there are a few metres to spin the legs then it's straight up the steep kick of May Hill that leads you to the Hairpin bend which, like all features on the TT route, has its own sign. Ride through and climb hard to the Waterworks Corner at which point you are already way above Ramsey and heading higher. The slope backs off for a while but soon comes back to bite you, through a right-hand bend, round this and the next left and your goal, Snaefell Mountain, comes into view. From here you can engage the big ring and pick up speed, it's still a long way, though. You must round the tip of the mountain, cross the tourist railway line in a small hollow then push it upwards to the point after which you can go no higher, at the sign for Hailwood's Height.

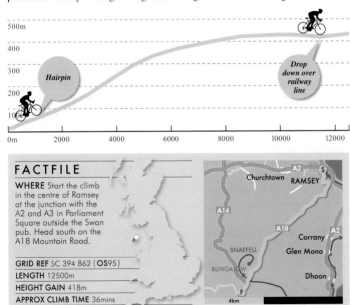

Hairpin

Drop down over railway line

FACTFILE

WHERE Start the climb in the centre of Ramsey at the junction with the A2 and A3 in Parliament Square outside the Swan pub. Head south on the A18 Mountain Road.

GRID REF SC 394 862 (**OS**95)

LENGTH 12500m

HEIGHT GAIN 418m

APPROX CLIMB TIME 36mins

HERE'S THE NEXT 100

So you've ridden all the hills in book one, it's dog-eared and ragged after a couple of years in your jersey pocket, and you're now at a loss. You need more goals? Where do you head to next? Well, just in time, here's your brand spanking new checklist just begging to be filled in. Here's the next set of climbs, the next set of monuments to work into your weekend adventures and evening training rides.

For those of you, however, who haven't finished book one yet, don't fear. Barring any monumental tectonic activity the roads aren't going anywhere so you've all the time in the world. I hope you enjoy this next 100 as much as the first. Thanks, and good luck.

SOUTH-WEST

No	Hill	Date Ridden	Time
101	Gold Hill		
102	Zig Zag Hill		
103	Park Hill		
104	Frocester Hill		
105	Bushcombe Lane		
106	Haresfield Beacon		
107	Symonds Yat		
108	Shaft Road		
109	Vale Street		
110	Countisbury Hill		
111	Millook		
112	Clovelly		
113	Bishop's Wood		
114	Talland Hill		

SOUTH-EAST

No	Hill	Date Ridden	Time
115	Ashdown Forest		
116	Combe Lane		
117	Chalkpit Lane		
118	Coldharbour Lane		

CHECKLIST

No	Hill	Date Ridden	Time
119	Quell Lane		
120	Barhatch Lane		
121	Dragon Hill Road		
122	Kingston Hill		
123	Down Lane		

EAST			
No	Hill	Date Ridden	Time
124	Watson's Hill		
125	Beacon Hill		

MIDLANDS			
No	Hill	Date Ridden	Time
126	Mam Tor		
127	Beeley Moor		
128	Burbage Moor		
129	Slack Hill		
130	Axe Edge		
131	Larkstone Lane		
132	Gun Hill		
133	The Wrekin		
134	Asterton Bank		
135	Clee Hill		
136	Edge Hill		

YORKSHIRE			
No	Hill	Date Ridden	Time
137	Ewden Bank		
138	Cragg Vale		
139	Mytholm Steeps		
140	Thwaites Brow		
141	Hainworth Lane		
142	Turf Moor		
143	Bowland Knotts		
144	Greets Moss		
145	Trapping Hill		

No	Hill	Date Ridden	Time
146	Nought Bank Road		
147	Sleights Moor		
148	Blakey Bank		
149	Caper Hill		
150	Egton High Moor		
151	Hanging Grimston		

NORTH-EAST			
No	Hill	Date Ridden	Time
152	Yad Moss		
153	Cuthbert's Hill		
154	Peat Hill		
155	Unthank Bank		
156	High Knowes		
157	Cragpit Hill		
158	Ryal's Hill		
159	Silverhills		

SCOTLAND			
No	Hill	Date Ridden	Time
160	Devil's Beef Tub		
161	Crow Road		
162	Duke's Pass		
163	Bealach Maim		
164	Glen Finart		
165	Glen Quaich		
166	Bealach Feith Nan Laogh		
167	Ben Lawers		
168	Glen Coe		
169	Bealach Ratagan		
170	Quiraing		

NORTH-WEST			
No	Hill	Date Ridden	Time
171	Pym Chair		
172	Knott Hill Lane		

173	Chew Road		
174	Crown Point		
175	Whalley Nab		
176	Newton Fell		
177	White Shaw Moss		
178	Bank House Moor		
179	Kiln Bank Cross		
180	Burn Edge		
181	The Struggle		
182	Blae Tarn		
183	Shot Moss		
184	Dowgang Hush		
185	Killhope Cross		
186	Great Dun Fell		

WALES

No	Hill	Date Ridden	Time
187	Long mountain		
188	Melin-y-Wig		
189	Llanberis Pass		
190	Prenteg		
191	Hirnant Pass		
192	Dyfi Forest		
193	Heol Senni		
194	Gospel Pass		
195	Gammalt		
196	Caerphilly Mountain		
197	Rhiwr Road		

ISLE OF MAN

No	Hill	Date Ridden	Time
198	Bungalow		
199	Injebreck Hill		
200	Snaefell Mountain		

WWW.100CLIMBS.CO.UK

THANK YOU

Thank you again firstly to my wife Charlotte and daughter Lux for putting up with 'ANOTHER' 100 Climbs, yes I know I said we were going to the beach on holiday – next year, I promise. Thanks to my parents for letting me just turn up and take their car at the drop of a hat, and for making sure I had enough supplies for my trips into the wilderness. To Nick Burton for his support throughout the project, for suffering up the hills and being the best wing man a hill climber could ask for. Thanks to my sister Clara and her husband Brian for putting me up, and again for double-checking all my maps. If you find a mistake, let me know and I'll give you their number. Since the launch of volume one I've had so much support, so many kind words that it's impossible to list everyone who's helped along the way and I apologize if I forget anyone, but here goes.

Thanks to all at *Cycling Weekly* for their continued support, especially Simon Richardson, Penny Commis and Luke Evans. To Claire Beaumont at Condor Cycles and to Paul and Caspar at Rollapaluza for staging the fantastic Urban Hill Climb up Swains Lane that helped launch Volume One. Thanks to Andy Waterman and Stuart Clapp, and Simon Gilbert at Garmin for sorting me out with a fantastic gadget and dragging me kicking and screaming into the 21st century. Thanks to Garry Becket, Paul Lofthouse, Tejvan Pettinger, Keith Bingham and Phil O'Conner. To James Dowd, Allen Bridge at Polocini, Talisker whisky and Jason Humphries for getting me started with the website. Thanks to Frances Lincoln for everything they have done to help make it all happen and *Amateur Photographer* magazine for keeping me in steady employment. To all the people who took flyers from me as I ran up and down hills with my home-made *100 Climbs* sign and to all those organisers who let me stick posters up at their events.

And last but certainly not least, a massive massive thank you to everyone who bought volume one. To everyone who left such wonderful feedback and to those who've written such fantastic reviews or tweeted their support. The response has been overwhelming and I hope you like this book just as much as the first. Thanks very much.

THE END